The Runner's SOURCEBOOK

Ellen E. Sampson

2168   1578

ROXBURY PARK

LOWELL HOUSE
LOS ANGELES

NTC/Contemporary Publishing Group

East Baton Rouge Parish Library
Baton Rouge, Louisiana

Library of Congress Cataloging-in-Publication Data

Sampson, Ellen.
    The runner's sourcebook / Ellen Sampson.
        p   cm.
    Includes bibliographical references and index.
    ISBN 1-56565-963-5 (alk. paper)
        1. Running Handbooks, manuals, etc. 2. Runners (Sports)
    Handbooks, manuals, etc. I. Title.
    GV1061.S26   1999
    796.42—dc21   99-22117
                                                             CIP

Published by Lowell House
A division of NTC/Contemporary Publishing Group, Inc.
4255 West Touhy Avenue, Lincolnwood (Chicago), Illinois 60646-1975 U.S.A.

© Copyright 1999 by Ellen E. Sampson
Cover photograph copyright © 1997 Bill Ling/Telegraph Colour
Library/FPG International LLC.

All rights reserved. No part of this book may be reproduced, stored in a
retrieval system, or transmitted in any form or by any means, electronic,
mechanical, photocopying, recording, or otherwise, without the prior permission of NTC/Contemporary Publishing Group, Inc.

Lowell House books can be purchased at special discounts when ordered in
bulk for premiums and special sales. Contact Department CS at the following address:
    NTC/Contemporary Publishing Group
    4255 West Touhy Avenue
    Lincolnwood, IL 60646-1975
    1-800-323-4900

Roxbury Park is a division of NTC/Contemporary Publishing Group, Inc.

Managing Director and Publisher: Jack Artenstein
Editor in Chief, Roxbury Park Books: Michael Artenstein
Director of Publishing Services: Rena Copperman
Editorial Assistant: Nicole Monastirsky
Interior Designer: Andrea Reider

Printed and bound in the United States of America
99 00 01 02 VP 10 9 8 7 6 5 4 3 2 1

Note to the Reader

The ideas, suggestions, and techniques in this book are not intended as a substitute for medical or other professional advice applicable to specific individuals. Consult with a physician or other qualified professional regarding your exercise or activity program.

This book is dedicated to my dad,
whose death from heart failure at the age of forty-one
prompted me to stay healthy through exercise.

Contents

Acknowledgments

While running down the road of life, literally and figuratively speaking, I've met many wonderful people who became my mentors, friends, and running partners. Their help and support enabled me to step off the beaten path and blaze my own trail.

Special thanks to Jeff Galloway and Sally Edwards for continually sharing their wisdom and expertise about health, fitness, business, and life.

To the love of my life, Bob Venditti; my best friend, Charlis McKay; my sister, Francis Pease; and my mom, Betty Sampson. They keep me grounded and offer helping hands without being asked.

To my literary agent, Nancy Crossman, my copyeditor Janet Byron, and Roxbury Park/Lowell House and Contemporary Books for giving me the opportunity to share my passion for running.

And to all the runners, walkers, and others who contributed in some way to this book including Bob and Jean Anderson, Noel Dybdal, Diane Etheridge, Allen and Lynda Estes, Lisa Glaser, Joe Henderson, Jeanette Link, Gary Moran, Lynn Yamamoto, and the folks at Fleet Feet.

Introduction

Welcome to *The Runner's Sourcebook* and the exciting and fun-filled world of running. As a nonrunner a decade ago, I never dreamed that any activity could have such a profound impact on so many aspects of my life. My running started out as just another form of exercise, like bicycling or swimming. With time and experience, it became my avocation, my occupation, and my passion.

During the 1970s, when the first running boom hit the United States, some of you were a part of it, training hard and racing hard. During this era, the likes of Jim Fixx, Frank Shorter, Kathrine Switzer, Steve Prefontaine, and many others began etching their places into American running history.

We are now knee-deep in the second running boom, although some people would argue the first one never ended. This time around you won't recognize most of the names associated with it except your own.

Today, many people who let the first boom cruise by unnoticed are lacing up their shoes and stepping out for the first time in middle age and even old age. Burned-out runners, who left the sport when chronic injuries or time constraints forced retirement, are returning to a kinder, gentler sport which now offers something for all ages and levels of ability and commitment. And, of course, a whole new generation of kids, teens, and young adults is discovering the joys of running.

Compared to the 1970s and 1980s, running is now a little less about competition and winning and more about health and fitness and having fun. Although competitive goals and personal records still guide many runners in their training and racing, there are just as many recreational and fitness runners who never step up to a starting line.

Whether you're a runner-to-be, a veteran runner, or a revitalized runner returning to the sport after an absence, *The Runner's Sourcebook* will get you off on the right foot for running in the new millennium. Its up-to-date information will serve as a valuable resource for all types of runners.

There aren't nearly enough pages for *The Runner's Sourcebook* to be an all-out training and racing book so I haven't tried to make it one. Besides, dozens of good running books have already been written (and you'll find some of them listed at the close of each chapter). Think of *The Runner's Sourcebook* as a hybrid—part how-to and part reference and resource. It explores running from various perspectives including health and fitness, recreation, and competition. In addition to providing all of the basic information you'll need to get acquainted with this diverse sport, the book includes numerous resources for obtaining more comprehensive and specific information.

You'll learn about running from all caliber of runners including respected running authorities such as Jeff Galloway, a 1972 Olympian, and *Runner's World* magazine columnist Joe Henderson, who has written nearly two dozen running books. Some real-life runners of various ages and abilities also share their own experiences and expertise.

Like many of you, my own running career started with a new pair of shoes and the desire to participate in a local 10-K fun run. It was the mid-1980s and at thirty-something I was determined to try this sport called "jogging." Lacking any natural talent or knowledge, I trained haphazardly, walking at first and eventually running more than I walked. Not knowing any other runners initially, I learned about the sport by the seat of my pants. (Actually, it was the soles of my shoes!)

My formal education and training as a runner began several years later at Jeff Galloway's running camp in Squaw Valley, California. Eager to learn as much as possible, I absorbed every word spoken by Jeff, his wife Barbara, and the other instructors. It was there, running trails in the majestic serenity of the Sierra Nevada wilderness, that I fell in love with running. Many of the words of running wisdom I heard that summer and in subsequent summers are found on the pages that follow.

Having completed twelve marathons and countless shorter races including one 5-K on snowshoes, my days as a neophyte runner are behind me, but not forgotten. In many ways, I continue to relive my early experiences vicariously through the men and women who participate in my new-runner classes and the Galloway training program I direct in Sacramento, California. Although I'll never meet the many runners who read and use *The Runner's Sourcebook*, I hope it will educate, motivate, and inspire you to run and walk wherever life takes you.

ELLEN E. SAMPSON

CHAPTER ONE

Running for the Health (and Fun) Of It

For millions of people of all ages, running is an integral part of their lives. It's the sport of choice for the individual and the group, the fast and the not-so-fast, the exerciser and the competitor, the unknown and the well-known. There are lots of runners and they're in good company; three recent U.S. presidents—Clinton, Bush, and Carter—are counted among their ranks.

A GROWING SPORT

According to the Sporting Goods Manufacturers Association, which tracks the fitness movement, running/jogging was one of the top five fitness activities in the United States during 1997. Their research shows that more than eight million Americans ran or jogged more than 100 days during 1997. The Road Running Information Center (RRIC) of the United States of America Track and Field (USAT&F), which governs road running and track-and-field events, reports that more than six million runners finished a road race during 1997. The numbers are growing.

THE CHANGING FACE OF RUNNING

A sport once dominated by young men, running has changed a lot since organized running races began in the United States during the nineteenth century. Most notably, women, who for the most part were excluded from the sport (by rules and attitudes) until the second half of the twentieth century, are now making up for lost time.

Henley Gabeau, executive director of the Road Runners Club of America (RRCA), a national association of 630 not-for-profit running clubs and their 180,000 members, recalls a time less than twenty years ago when virtually all running-club presidents were men, and women comprised only a quarter of the RRCA membership. Today, she says, most clubs have equal numbers of men and women and many of the presidents are women.

A steady influx of women into the sport has contributed significantly to record numbers of participants in road racing events. "The sport has become mainstream," says Ryan Lamppa of USAT&F/RRIC. "It has crossed the spectrum of all Americans."

Lamppa also attributes continually increasing participation to the introduction of cause-oriented events such as the Susan G. Komen Breast Cancer Foundation's Race for the Cure, new group-training programs, and more events aimed at families. And, not only are more people racing than ever before, Lamppa says, but aging baby boomers are taking better care of themselves and they keep on running and racing.

Running has not been without its critics over the years. Prior to and around the turn of the twentieth century, many doctors were opposed to vigorous exercise and athletics. Medical journals of the day referred to a condition called "athlete's heart," which was characterized by lower resting heart rates, murmurs, enlarged hearts, and irregular heartbeats. The very same symptoms we accept as normal for high-performance athletes today indicated a diseased heart in a different era.

Eventually many of the early theories and ideas became discredited as researchers and doctors began exploring the relationship of exercise to health and longevity.

Today, the evidence is clear. Lack of physical activity is a major risk factor for heart disease. Regular aerobic exercise, like running, can lead to a healthier, happier, longer life. We also know that many of the physiological declines generally associated with aging are the result of inactivity and disuse, not old age. Research now supports the old adage, "Use it or lose it."

WHY DO RUNNERS RUN?

In one recent survey of almost a thousand runners, nearly all indicated that they run to keep in shape and more than 90 percent said they like the mental benefits. Other top reasons for running included to relieve stress and control weight.

There are many more good reasons to exercise and run. The mental and physical benefits alone are numerous. By eating a healthy diet and adopting a regular running and fitness routine, you can expect:

- Increased energy and stamina.
- Improved bone density and lower risk of osteoporosis.
- Stronger cardiovascular, respiratory, muscular, and skeletal systems.
- Improved self-esteem, body image, and confidence.
- Reduced body fat and improved weight control.
- Lower risk of heart disease.
- Less stress, anxiety, and depression.
- Improved sleeping habits.
- Lower blood pressure and lower cholesterol.
- Increased life expectancy.

Other sports offer many of the same health benefits, but running burns the most calories (nearly twice as many as walking) and can improve cardiovascular fitness much faster. Although many people start running for health, they keep running because it's convenient, inexpensive, rewarding, fun, and . . . the list continues.

Running is easy and doesn't take special skills or equipment. It's both a solitary sport and a group activity which can be done anytime and anywhere. It also runs the gamut from simple exercise to a diverse, competitive sporting event. Any person can find a niche in running, regardless of their shape, age, ability, level of interest, and goals. As chapters four and twelve discuss, there are many different ways to experience and enjoy running.

Running offers an opportunity rarely found in other sports—ordinary runners can mix with world-class athletes. "You can't play in the Super Bowl or the NBA play-offs," Don Kardong writes in the RRCA booklet *Why Run? Running for Health, Fun and Fitness,* "but on almost every weekend runners compete in the same events with the fastest human beings ever to inhabit the planet."

He adds that many runners who begin to get in shape later find that racing is great motivation to continue. For those who aren't interested in the competitive aspect of running, Kardong notes, "There are low-key social events that emphasize fun and friendship."

BENEFITS OF RUNNING OUTWEIGH RISKS

Does running competitively or recreationally have a downside or present any potential risks? Of course, doesn't everything? Muscle or joint injuries are the most likely possibility and in rare circumstances, hidden health problems may become evident; never ignore mild symptoms, which may indicate more serious health concerns. Runners have also been known to become so compulsive about running (seriously) that they begin to ignore other important aspects of their lives, such as family.

Most runners will agree that the benefits of running and exercise outweigh any potential risks or negative impacts. You can reduce the likelihood of serious health problems by making sure it's safe to start running and checking with a health practitioner if you suspect something's wrong. To avoid compulsive running, keep balance in your life. Even positive behaviors like running can become unhealthy if done to excess.

STARTING OUT MAY REQUIRE A CHECKUP

If you are new to running or exercise, you may wonder whether to consult a doctor before getting started. The answer depends on a number of factors including your age, health, current level of fitness, and the intensity of running you intend to do. Running is generally considered a vigorous activity and as such should be approached more cautiously than a low-to-moderate intensity activity like walking.

If you are a female under the age of fifty or a male under the age of forty and in good health, exercise is probably safe for you.

GENERAL GUIDELINES
TO CONSIDER BEFORE RUNNING

In its 1996 exercise guidelines, which are considered a model for the health-and-fitness industry, the American College of Sports Medicine (ACSM) recommends that men above the age of forty and women above the age of fifty should have a medical examination and a clinical exercise test before beginning a vigorous exercise program.

At any age, the American Council on Exercise advises to check with a doctor if you have two or more of the coronary artery disease (CAD) risk factors listed below.

Coronary Artery Disease Risk Factors

- Family history of heart attack or sudden death
- Age (women >55 and men >45)
- Physically inactive
- Smoke cigarettes
- High blood pressure
- Diabetes
- High cholesterol

Are you still uncertain? Review the following checklist developed by the National Institutes of Health (NIH), and mark any items that apply to you.

- ☐ Your doctor said you have a heart condition and recommended only medically supervised physical activity.
- ☐ During or right after exercise, you frequently have pains or pressure in the left- or mid-chest area, or the left neck, shoulder or arm.
- ☐ You have developed chest pain within the last month.
- ☐ Your doctor recommended you take medicine for your blood pressure or a heart condition.
- ☐ You tend to lose consciousness or fall over due to dizziness.
- ☐ Your doctor said you have bone or joint problems that could be made worse by the proposed physical activity.
- ☐ You feel extremely breathless after mild exertion.
- ☐ You are middle-aged or older, have not been physically active, and plan a relatively vigorous exercise program.
- ☐ You have a medical condition or other physical reason not mentioned here which might need special attention in an exercise program (for example, insulin-dependent diabetes).

NIH recommends seeing your doctor before starting to exercise if you've checked one or more items. If no items are checked, NIH recommends starting on a gradual, sensible program of increased activity tailored to your needs.

Additionally, NIH makes one caveat. If you feel any of the physical symptoms listed above when you start your exercise program, contact your doctor right away.

If it's safe for you to start running, turn the page and gear up to run.

RESOURCES

For entertaining and inspirational running fiction, humor, biographies, essays, and poems read:

Battista, Garth, compiler. *The Runner's Literary Companion: Great Stories and Poems About Running.* New York: Breakaway Books, 1994.

Bingham, John. *The Courage to Start: A Guide to Running for Your Life.* New York: Fireside/Simon & Schuster, 1999.

Burfoot, Amby. *The Principles of Running: Practical Lessons from My First 100,000 Miles.* Emmaus, Pa.: Rodale Press, 1999.

Galloway, Jeff. *Return of the Tribes to Peachtree Street.* Atlanta, Ga.: Phidippides Publicaion, 1995.

Henderson, Joe. *Did I Win? A Farewell to George Sheehan.* Waco, Tex.: WRS Publishing, 1995.

Parker, John L. Jr. *Once a Runner.* Rev. ed., Tallahassee, Fla.: Cedarwinds Publishing, 1999.

Pont, Sally. *Finding Their Stride.* Orlando, Fla.: Harcourt Brace, 1999.

Will-Weber, Mark; ed. *The Quotable Runner.* New York: Breakaway Books, 1995.

To find or start a running club in your area:

Road Runners Club of America (RRCA)
1150 S. Washington St., #250
Alexandria, VA 22314
Phone: (703) 836-0558
Fax: (703) 836-4430
E-mail: office@rrca.org
Web site: www.rrca.org

To join a virtual running club or team go to:

Clydesdale Virtual Running Team (large runners): www.cvrt.org
Dead Runner's Society: http://storm.cadcam.iupui.edu/drs/drs
John Bingham's Team Penguin: www.waddle-on.com
Team Clydesdale (large runners): www.teamclydesdale.com

To find out about the local running scene in your community visit your closest running store or subscribe to one of the many national, regional, or local running publications (see the appendix).

CHAPTER TWO

Gearing Up To Run

Unlike many sports that require an array of expensive equipment and gear from the get-go, you can take your first running steps wearing everyday items found in your closet. As you continue running on a regular basis, you'll soon appreciate why special attire and accessories were created specifically for the sport.

Most casual footwear and apparel are not designed for regular use during a vigorous exercise like running. Basketball and tennis shoes, for example, lack the essential cushioning runners need. Everyday shorts are usually too long to provide the full range of running motion. And many casual T-shirts and other clothing items are not made of fabrics that will keep you cool and dry when you work up a good sweat.

You don't need to spend a lot of money on running gear but you do need to buy a few key items. If you run several days a week, the money you spend on good running shoes, appropriate running attire, and a few accessories will be well worth the investment. Take the time to evaluate your own individual needs and preferences. What works for one runner may not work for you.

STEPPING OUT IN THE RIGHT SHOES AND SOCKS

Feet come in all shapes and sizes and move in different ways as they hit and leave the ground with each step. While they're not much to look at, feet are truly remarkable. They support and propel the body, and provide balance. Your feet can also tolerate a great deal of impact during exercise.

When you run, twenty-six little bones, thirty-three joints, and a network of tendons, muscles, and ligaments in each foot are forced to absorb shock and support up to three times your body weight. For a 150-pound runner on a three-mile run, the cumulative impact on each foot is more than 150 tons. The right shoes can give your feet a helping hand by absorbing that shock and providing necessary support.

What is the Best Shoe for Running?

A running shoe! This might sound elementary, but every year dozens of marathoners-to-be show up on the first day of training wearing shoes designed for some other sport. If you are going to run, wear a running shoe. If you are going to walk and run, also wear a running shoe.

What about cross-training shoes? Cross-trainers have been aptly described by some salespeople as "the shoes that do nothing well." Cross-training shoes are adequate for ten miles per week or less, but running shoes are always preferable.

Choose Function, not Fad or Fashion

After narrowing down the choice to running shoes, there are still more than a dozen major manufacturers and countless models or styles with fancy features ranging from grids and gels to pods and plugs. Don't make the mistake of picking a shoe by the color, look, or even the brand. Always buy running shoes for their function, not fashion or fad. Your shoes should match your running needs, foot type, and biomechanics.

If new to running, get off on the right foot by shopping at an athletic store that specializes in running shoes. Plan to spend at least thirty minutes getting analyzed and trying on several models and sizes. A knowledgeable salesperson at any reputable store will start by asking you a few questions.

Pat Sweeney, owner of Fleet Feet Sports in downtown Sacramento, California, says at his store (and some thirty Fleet Feet stores throughout the United States) you can expect to be asked the following questions:

- Do you run now? If so, how many miles per week?
- How often do you run and on what kinds of surfaces?
- What shoe do you run in?
- Have you had any injuries?
- What type of training do you intend to do?

Be prepared to answer these types of questions. If a salesperson doesn't ask something similar, leave and go to a store where they do. You can also expect to have the salesperson look at your shoe-less feet, examine your old shoes, and watch as you run up and down the aisle or sidewalk.

"Don't worry," says Diane Etheridge, manager of Phidippides, an Atlanta, Georgia, running store. "We're only looking at your feet from the ankles down." By determining your foot type and what the foot does when it hits and leaves the ground, she explains, it's easier for a salesperson to narrow the selection to shoes with certain characteristics that fit you and your budget.

For example, flat feet need a shoe with motion control. A curved foot with a high arch, on the other hand, usually requires more cushioning. Review the glossary included in this chapter to become more familiar with common terms that apply to shoes and feet.

THE WET TEST

Do you know whether you have high, medium, or low arches? Take the "Wet Test" and find out. Wet the bottoms of your bare feet and then walk on a hard surface, like dry cement. Now, match your footprints to the examples shown on the next page. Keep in mind that your arch is just one of several characteristics to consider when selecting shoes.

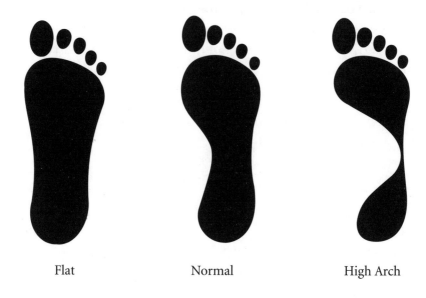

| Flat | Normal | High Arch |

Some of the larger retail sports chains now offer electronic foot scanners and treadmills with cameras to videotape customers as they walk and run. While high tech has some advantages, many multisport megastores do not offer personalized customer service and in all likelihood their salespeople don't even run. Local running specialty stores, on the other hand, are usually staffed by runners and the store supports the running community by distributing race information and sponsoring special events for runners such as races, training programs, and clinics. Patronize these stores; the personal attention is well worth the few dollars you may save at a large, chain sporting-goods store.

Comfort is Critical

Although the salesperson can tell which shoes meet your needs and budget, only you know how the shoes feel. Comfort and fit are essential considerations, so don't fret if the size is much larger than your street shoes. Running shoes should be comfortable from the moment you put them on. They won't stretch out or "break in." Do, however, ease into wearing a new pair of shoes by using them on a few short runs before trying a long run. The shoe and your foot may need time to adapt to each other. Many runners like alternating different pairs of shoes. This practice gives each pair a chance to dry out between runs. You can also be more specific about your needs, selecting a heavier, cushioned shoe for long runs and a lighter one for short, everyday runs.

While it may seem expensive the first time around, consider buying a second pair when your first pair still has about half of its life. That way you can ease into the new pair gradually and always have an extra pair on hand.

Get a Good Fit

To get a good fit, the American Orthopaedic Foot and Ankle Society, a group of medical doctors specializing in foot care, recommends that you:

- Visit the shoe store at the end of a workout when your feet are largest.
- Wear the socks you normally wear when working out.
- Fit the shoe to the largest foot.
- Make sure you can wiggle all your toes freely.
- Allow at least one thumb's width of space from the longest toe to the end of the toe box (when standing).
- Put your orthotics (if you wear any) in shoes you are fitting.

Selecting shoes does get easier once you begin to understand basic terminology and your own biomechanics. Listen carefully each time a shoe specialist recommends one type of shoe over another. Most of the information won't sink in at first but it will after buying a few pairs of shoes. Eventually, you'll walk into the store with confidence and say something like, "I need a stable training shoe with a wide toe box in about a size eight."

MAIL-ORDER SHOE EXPERTS

When buying shoes, there is no substitute for having knowledgeable shoe personnel watch you run, look at your feet, and examine your shoes. If you're unable to locate a running specialty store in your area, there are several options.

Road Runner Sports A mail-order company based in San Diego, California, offers an analysis clinic to help select the right shoes for your individual needs and style of running. For a fee, they'll examine the worn shoes you send in their postage-paid envelope, review your answers to a detailed questionnaire, and make a recommendation.

The American Running and Fitness Association A nonprofit educational organization of runners, also maintains a running-shoe database to help its members (nonmembers pay a fee) find running shoes that match their individual needs. After completing a questionnaire, the runner receives a personalized listing of appropriate shoes, suggested retail prices, and the name and phone number of the manufacturer.

Wear May Not be Evident

To get the full benefit of owning a good pair of shoes, care for them properly and replace them regularly. Most moderate-to-higher priced running shoes will last for three hundred to five hundred miles, if used exclusively for running. Your weight, running style, exposure to the weather, and other factors will influence their longevity. Keep track of the mileage on your shoes by writing it in your workout log. Some runners use a permanent-ink marker to write the purchase date on the outside or inside of their shoes.

You *can't* always identify excessive wear by a shoe's appearance. Shoes can be long past their prime and still "look" new. If a new injury or pain surfaces when your training has remained constant or increased gradually, broken-down shoes may be to blame. In the long run, new shoes are much cheaper than doctor appointments.

Don't Cook Your Shoes

Heat doesn't mix well with athletic shoes. "Nothing will shorten the life of your shoes faster than exposing them to the high temperatures like the trunk of your car," notes J. D. Denton, a running-magazine columnist who is known to his readers as "The Shoe Guy."

"You might as well just put them in the microwave. If you wouldn't leave your dog in the car, don't leave your shoes."

The glue that holds shoes together, Denton explains, is heat-activated and breaks down at high temperatures. That's also one reason why cleaning shoes in the washing machine and clothes dryer is never recommended. If your shoes do get wet, Denton suggests stuffing them with crumpled newspaper and placing them away from direct sunlight or any other heat source. Replace the paper periodically until the shoes are dry.

Socks

The issue of socks is a very personal one. Some people like runner/writer Joe Henderson run *au naturel* (without socks) while others like piles of cushioning between their shoes and feet. For most veteran runners, finding the right sock is a process of trial and error. Thankfully, the staple 100 percent cotton socks of yesteryear have long since been replaced with synthetic ones, which boast an array of "moisture management" characteristics. When cotton gets wet from sweaty feet or the elements, it stays that way and the resulting friction causes blisters and chafing.

Socks should keep your feet cool, dry, and blister-free. Most of the new human-made fibers will do that. Select your sock size carefully so that they fit your feet smoothly without folds or wrinkles. Although a few crew-length socks are still available on the market, the shorter, ankle-high styles are currently the most popular. Style and length are not as important as finding a sock that hugs your ankle snugly without sliding into the shoe as you run. Consider wearing taller socks if you run where poison oak or other irritating plants and ticks can be found.

SPEAKING OF SHOES

Board-lasted Full length of cardboardlike material glued to the *midsole,* which can contribute to stability.

Combination-lasted Cardboardlike material in the heel and stitching of the forefoot which provides stability in the rearfoot and flexibility in the forefoot.

Cushioning The shoe's ability to absorb the shock or impact of the foot as it touches then leaves the ground.

Foot biomechanics Study of the foot's movement and force.

Heel counter Rigid shoe piece that surrounds the heel and holds it steady.

Insole Removable pad found inside the shoe. Also known as *sockliner.*

Last A foot-shaped form on which a shoe is constructed. A shoe's last can be identified by removing its *insole* or *sockliner.*

Midsole Synthetic material located between the *outsole* and *insole,* which can dictate the shoe's function including cushioning, shock absorption, flexibility, and stability.

Motion control Shoe's ability to limit or "control" excessive inward roll of the foot *(overpronation).* Also see *stability.*

Orthotics or **Orthoses** In-shoe devices designed to provide relief to a particular area of the foot while supporting other areas. Custom-made inserts are available with a prescription and simple models can be purchased over-the-counter.

Outsole Bottom of the shoe which touches the ground. It provides traction, resists wear, and can contribute to shock absorption.

Overpronation Excessive inward roll of the foot before push-off.

Pronation or **Neutral pronation** Natural, normal motion when the foot rolls inward then flattens out before toeing off. It absorbs the shock of impact and allows the body and feet to adapt to different surfaces.

Shape Contour of a shoe that dictates how it fits the contour of the foot. The three basic shoe shapes are straight, curved, and semicurved. Semicurved is most common because it accommodates the widest variety of foot types.

Slip-lasted Stitching which runs down the middle of the entire length of the shoe making it very flexible.

Sockliner See *insole.*

Stability A shoe's ability to resist excessive foot motion. See *motion control.*

Supination or **Underpronation** Uncommon motion when the foot rolls outward, usually indicating a stable foot.

Toebox Part of the *upper* around the toes.

Upper Entire top of the shoe.

DRESSING FOR RUNNING SUCCESS

Apparel Basics

Like shoes, running clothes should be selected for function and comfort. The colors, patterns, and styles will change from season to season, but in the end you'll only wear the items that fit and feel good while running.

During fair weather, shorts, shirt, and a sports bra (for women), make up the apparel basics. Extremely cold or wet conditions may require additional clothing such as tights, jackets, and wind suits. A sports watch (with or without heart monitor), sunglasses, gloves, hat, and a water bottle or pack complete the list of essential gear found in the closets of most avid runners.

Be Selective

Don't make the mistake of going out and buying all your running gear at one time. Add items as the need for them arises. With running experience, you will become more selective and better able to determine what items and features best meet your own individual needs and preferences.

Shorts. Running shorts are short for a reason; they allow the legs to move freely. Long shorts, with an inseam measurement of more than about four inches, have a tendency to ride up in the crotch area and restrict movement unless you have really long legs.

Two of the most common styles of shorts are the V-notch and half-split. The latter, as the name implies, splits up the side offering extra room for moving and a little less modesty than the V-notch. With very few exceptions, running shorts are made of quick-drying nylon or polyester with trade names such as CoolMax and Supplex. The most significant considerations in selecting shorts will be how much room and length you want. Most men's and women's running shorts include built-in briefs. As a personal preference, many runners add separate briefs or a supporter.

Some runners, including those with ample thighs, may prefer running in thigh-length fitness shorts, which look like bicycling pants without padding. Usually made of a stretchy fabric called Lycra, fitness shorts provide more support and warmth than running shorts and protect against inner-thigh chafing. There are a number of special runner's lubricants (Runner's Lube and Body Glide are two) which effectively reduce chafing from skin-to-skin or skin-to-clothing friction.

Shirts and tops. It doesn't take most runners very long to acquire a drawer full of cotton or cotton-blend race T-shirts, but many of those shirts end up as casual wear rather than running wear. This is particularly true in extremely hot or cold climates. During the winter, cotton shirts that get wet from perspiration or the elements stay wet and can give you a chill. In the summer, they keep your natural cooling system from functioning properly.

The best running tops, like socks, are made of fabrics that wick away moisture from the body. The choice of sleeve length will be dictated by the weather: long sleeves for cold weather, singlets or tank tops for warm weather, and short sleeves for moderate weather.

Sports bras. A relative newcomer to the running scene, sports bras are now available in a full range of colors, sizes, and support. Most models can be worn with or without a top. Again, like all running apparel, breathable, moisture-wicking fabrics are the most comfortable. A sports bra should fit snugly without riding up, binding, or restricting movement. Don't be afraid to run in place and jump around in the dressing room to evaluate a bra's support and comfort. Also look closely at the stitching and seams. Both features should feel soft and smooth to the touch or chafing may result.

Cold-weather apparel. Unless you live in a year-round mild climate or intend to run indoors during the winter, you will eventually want to invest in cold-weather running gear. It will protect you from the cold, wet, and wind and make running more enjoyable. "Invest" is the operative word here because the price of one jacket can easily cost more than a top-of-the-line running shoe. But there is a bright side. If you buy quality items and care for them according to the instructions, they will provide years of warmth and comfort.

In the days before synthetics, "bundle up" was the solution to inclement weather. Today, the answer to cold, wet, or windy conditions is "layer up." Depending upon the conditions, two to four layers on the upper body and one or two layers on the lower body are generally suggested.

According to runner and outdoor enthusiast Gary Noe, two layers are all most runners need to stay comfortable if they pick the right fibers or fabrics. "Cotton kills," Noe says. "Runners should always use synthetics." If you must wear a natural fiber, he recommends either silk or wool.

Unfortunately, Noe points out, running is an activity that produces a lot of heat, and perspiration can eventually overwhelm almost anything you wear. "You will get wet," he says, but high-tech, synthetic fabrics that absorb moisture and let it pass through from the inside out—called "wicking"—will keep you from getting too cold or chilled.

Always be sure the layer closest to the skin fits snugly and is made of polypropylene or polyester, which are often sold under trade names such as CoolMax, Radiator, and Dri-F.I.T.

The outside layer should be made of materials that will protect you from the elements. A windproof nylon shell or suit is best for windy days but you'll need something breathable and waterproof, such as a Gore-Tex top, for rainy days. On a cold, clear day, the second layer should insulate and provide warmth. A heavier wicking layer can serve that purpose if worn alone, worn over the inside layer, or added as the middle of three layers.

Noe also cautions runners to protect their hands, feet, and head. "A lot of your body heat goes out through your head, and your extremities are especially vulnerable to the cold," he says. A warm hat that covers the ears plus gloves (mittens are even better) will keep you toasty.

Accessories

If there's some item you think would improve your life as a runner, it can probably be found as a running accessory. If it doesn't hang on the wall or sit on the sales counter at the running store, it will likely be advertised in the back of running magazines and mail-order catalogs.

By adding the following accessories you will be all geared up to run day or night, in almost any weather.

- Sunglasses, sun visor, or cap
- Handheld water bottle or water pack/belt

THE TWENTY-DEGREE-FAHRENHEIT RULE

The key to dressing for running success is knowing how to dress for the weather. Overdressing or underdressing can be uncomfortable and even dangerous. By following the twenty-degree-Fahrenheit rule you can be comfortably dressed for all but very extreme conditions:

Dress for weather that is 20°F warmer than the actual outdoor temperature.

In other words, if the outdoor temperature is sixty degrees Fahrenheit, dress for eighty-degree weather. (When the temperature is measured in Celsius, follow a ten-degree rule.) You may feel a little underdressed when starting to run but after a few minutes your body will be comfortable. Additional tips for cold- and hot-weather running are included in chapter seven.

- Key pocket or carrier (for keys, identification, and cash)
- Reflective vest
- Sports watch and/or heart rate monitor

What are you waiting for? It's time to start running.

RESOURCES

For a free copy of *How to Select Sports Shoes* and/or *The Ten Points of Shoe Fit*, send a self-addressed, stamped envelope to:

American Orthopaedic Foot and Ankle Society
1216 Pine St., Suite 201
Seattle, WA 98101
Phone: 1-800-235-4855 or (206) 223-1120
Fax: (206) 223-1178
E-mail: aofas@aofas.org
Web site: www.aofas.org

For on-line links to many major running shoe and apparel companies, visit the Sporting Goods Manufacturers Association (SGMA) at www.sportlink.com.

Sporting Goods Manufacturers Association
200 Castlewood Dr.
North Palm Beach, FL 33418
Phone: (561) 842-4100
Fax: (561) 863-8984

CHAPTER THREE

Starting Out On the Right Foot

For runners-to-be and new runners, this chapter contains some of the most valuable information you will need. Even experienced runners can benefit from reviewing some of the beginning basics.

There is rarely a middle ground in people's opinions about running: either you love it or you hate it. Very few people will simply say, "It's OK." Many of the people who try running but quit within a month or two end up injured or aching from doing too much. Others drop out because it isn't fun for them or doesn't offer early rewards.

At a prerace clinic, four-time Olympian Francie Larrieu Smith, honorary chair of Race for the Cure, offered new runners some sound advice.

Larrieu Smith recounted the story of a former roommate who decided to take up running and did four miles the first day. She ran several more days in a row, and after the end of the first week the woman never took another running step. Larrieu Smith said her advice is the same for all runners-to-be, regardless of age: "Take it easy. You'll have more fun and you'll be more likely to stay with running."

Bill Rodgers espouses a similar message. In *Bill Rodgers' Lifetime Running Plan*, he states, "The advice I have for beginners is of the same philosophy that I have for runners of all levels of experience and ability—consistency, a sane approach, moderation, and making your running an enjoyable, rather than dreaded, part of your life."

If you hope to have a long career as a runner, get off to a good start by going easy, progressing gradually, and establishing good habits from the onset. A few select neophytes (particularly those under twenty-five with the right genes) can put on their first pair of running shoes, head out the door, and run to their heart's content from day one. For most of the rest of us, such zealousness can lead to early (and often chronic) injuries and frustration.

The human body, though remarkable by its very nature, isn't designed to create full-fledged runners in a week or two. As you'll learn later, an injury can develop for weeks or even months before you feel a significant pain. It doesn't matter whether you aspire to run around the block or qualify for the Boston Marathon, begin life as a runner by running regularly and adding to your running routine progressively. By gradually training your body to handle the demands of running, you will see more improvement and enjoy a longer and healthier life as a runner. Even a fit individual who trains in other sports should approach running conservatively in the beginning.

ANATOMY OF A RUNNING WORKOUT

Regardless of the activity, the anatomy of a workout is usually the same. There's a warm-up at the beginning, a cool-down at the end, and the "work" of the workout sandwiched in-between.

Warm-up

As a general rule of thumb, the warm-up should equal at least 10 percent of the total workout time and gently use your sport-specific muscles. For runners, warming up means walking or jogging slowly for a few minutes before running. The purpose of a warm-up is to gradually prepare the body for the higher-intensity "work" that will follow. A good warm-up will gently increase body temperature, respiration, and heart rate and make the run more comfortable. It will also reduce the risk of injury.

Cool-down

The cool-down functions in the reverse. It helps the body gradually return to its preexercise state, dissipate heat, and aid in the recovery of muscles. End your runs by gradually slowing the pace until it becomes a walk. Never stop running abruptly or sit down before your heart rate and breathing are back to normal. An inadequate cool-down may cause cramping, irregular heartbeats, muscle soreness, or more serious problems.

In most cases, a cool-down, like a warm-up, should last at least 10 percent of the workout time but not less than five minutes. The time, however, will vary according to the individual and the intensity of the workout. Beginning runners, in particular, may require a longer cool-down because their bodies aren't conditioned to recover as quickly as runners with higher levels of aerobic fitness.

Work

The "work" portion of a workout is designed to improve fitness by "overloading" the body or making it work harder than it is used to. As the body adapts to the new demands, the "training effect" occurs and fitness improves. The amount of overload required to maintain or improve fitness in a given sport is determined by three interrelated components—frequency, intensity, and time. Coaches and fitness professionals refer to them collectively as the F.I.T. Principle.

TO STRETCH OR NOT TO STRETCH?

Although opinions vary, it is often suggested that stretching or flexibility exercises be done as part of the warm-up or after a cool-down. You will have to decide what's best for you and your body. There is, however, general agreement that you should never stretch muscles that have not been warmed with mild activity. Specific information on stretching and examples of useful running stretches are in chapter six.

F = Frequency or How Often to Run

You must run regularly to improve fitness and running ability. However, the conventional running wisdom that "more is better" has lost some of its popularity, and has been replaced with the ideal that consistency and "quality" miles, not "quantity," will foster improved running performance and reduce the risk of injury.

For the beginning runner, three days of running each week will provide significant conditioning without the risk of injury or burnout. Running less than three days a week offers very little improvement, while injuries increase drastically for those who run more than four or five days a week. To achieve additional benefits without risking injury, other forms of exercise can be done on non-running days.

I = Intensity or How Hard to Work Out

Your running pace for the first few months should allow you to carry on a comfortable conversation. If you can pass this "talk test," you are probably running aerobically and your heart rate is less than 75 percent of its maximum. By definition, "aerobic" means that oxygen is present. By running aerobically, you are training your heart, lungs, and circulatory system to function efficiently and provide the working muscles with needed oxygen.

If breathing is difficult, you won't be able to maintain that pace for long because the body can no longer meet its demand for oxygen. At that point, anaerobic (without oxygen) metabolism predominates and rapid fatigue follows. A burning sensation in the muscles is another sign that you are running too hard.

Many beginning runners fail the talk test repeatedly and eventually fall victim to the "terrible too's." By running too hard, too fast, too far, too soon when the body isn't prepared for the stress, it doesn't have enough time to recover and breaks down. Constant fatigue or aches and pains make running a lot less enjoyable and satisfying.

All runners—novices and veterans—achieve at different levels based on various factors including genetics, age, cardiovascular endurance, overall fitness, and experience. Depending on the individual runner, the same nine-minute-per-mile pace may be a warm-up, a workout, or a race. As a beginner, it is better to err on the side of taking it too easy. Don't pick some arbitrary pace and try to maintain it. Just run comfortably and let your body determine the pace.

T = Time or How Long to Work Out

Exercise must last a certain length of time for specific benefits to occur. For cardiovascular endurance in high-intensity activities like running, a minimum of about twenty minutes is required. You can also develop cardiovascular endurance during low-intensity activities like brisk walking, but you must exercise much longer for the same benefit.

The goal of any beginning runner should be to develop enough cardiovascular endurance to easily sustain a running workout without a great deal of fatigue or muscle soreness. As the heart and lungs develop, the body is also getting accustomed to the movement of running and the strain of a new weight-bearing activity.

During this initial stage, sometimes called "building base," your runs should be easy and enjoyable. This is an especially critical time in your development as a runner, if you have competitive goals. This base becomes the foundation for future strength building and speed training.

If you run long enough, you'll soon discover that for just about every piece of running advice you read or hear there is another recommendation that is entirely different. This is also true of training programs and racing schedules. When it comes to exercise (and running), one size doesn't fit all. The key is to identify and use workouts and training programs that meet your individual needs. With that in mind, here is a three-month program for beginners developed by the American Running and Fitness Association (ARFA).

EASY 12-WEEK WALK/RUN PROGRAM

	Day One	Day Two	Day Three	Day Four	Day Five	Day Six	Day Seven
1	Walk 15 min. Vary your pace. Try not to stop.	Walk 5 min. Run 1. (Repeat for a total of 17 min.) Walk 5.	Walk 15 min. Vary your pace. Try not to stop.	Walk 5 min. Run 1. (Repeat for a total of 17 min.) Walk 5.	Walk 15 min. Vary your pace. Try not to stop.	Walk 5 min. Run 1. (Repeat for a total of 17 min.) Walk 5.	Rest!
2	Walk 15 min. Run 1. Walk 2.	Walk 5 min. Run 3. (Repeat for a total of 21 min.) Walk 5.	Walk 15 min. Run 1. Walk 2.	Walk 5 min. Run 3. (Repeat for a total of 21 min.) Walk 5.	Walk 15 min. Run 1. Walk 2.	Walk 5 min. Run 3. (Repeat for a total of 21 min.) Walk 5.	Rest!
3	Walk 15 min. Run 1. Walk 2.	Walk 6 min. Run 4. (Repeat for a total of 26 min.) Walk 5.	Walk 15 min. Run 1. Walk 2.	Walk 6 min. Run 4. (Repeat for a total of 26 min.) Walk 5.	Walk 15 min. Run 1. Walk 2.	Walk 6 min. Run 4. (Repeat for a total of 26 min.) Walk 5.	Rest!
4	Walk 15 min. Run 2. Walk 4.	Walk 3 min. Run 2. (Repeat for a total of 30 min.) Walk 5.	Walk 15 min. Run 2. Walk 4.	Walk 3 min. Run 2. (Repeat for a total of 30 min.) Walk 5.	Walk 15 min. Run 2. Walk 4.	Walk 3 min. Run 2. (Repeat for a total of 30 min.) Walk 5.	Rest!
5	Walk 15 min. Run 2. Walk 4.	Walk 5 min. Run 5. (Repeat for a total of 35 min.) Walk 5.	Walk 15 min. Run 2. Walk 4.	Walk 5 min. Run 5. (Repeat for a total of 35 min.) Walk 5.	Walk 15 min. Run 2. Walk 4.	Walk 5 min. Run 5. (Repeat for a total of 35 min.) Walk 5.	Rest!

6	Walk 30 min.	Walk 4 min. Run 6. (Repeat twice.) Walk 5.	Walk 30 min.	Walk 4 min. Run 6. (Repeat twice.) Walk 5.	Walk 30 min.	Walk 4 min. Run 6. (Repeat twice.) Walk 5.	Rest!
7	Walk 30 min.	Walk 4 min. Run 6. (Repeat twice.) Walk 5.	Walk 5 min. Run 10. Walk 5.	Walk 2 min. Run 1. (Repeat 9 times.) Walk 5.	Walk 5 min. Run 10. Walk 5.	Walk 2 min. Run 1. (Repeat 9 times.) Walk 5.	Rest!
8	Walk 30 min.	Walk 2 min. Run 1. (Repeat 9 times.) Walk 5.	Walk 5 min. Run 15. Walk 5.	Walk 2 min. Run 1. (Repeat 9 times.) Walk 5.	Walk 5 min. Run 15. Walk 5.	Walk 1 min. Run 30 sec. (Repeat 20 times.) Walk 5.	Rest!
9	Walk 30 min.	Walk 1 min. Run 30 sec. (Repeat 20 times.) Walk 5.	Walk 5 min. Run 20. Walk 5.	Walk 1 min. Run 30 sec. (Repeat 20 times.) Walk 5.	Walk 5 min. Run 20. Walk 5.	Walk 1 min. Run 30 sec. (Repeat 20 times.) Walk 5.	Rest!
10	Walk 5 min. Run 20. Walk 5.	Walk 15.	Walk 5 min. Run 20. Walk 5.	Walk 15.	Walk 5 min. Run 20. Walk 5.	Walk 15 min.	Rest!
11	Walk 5 min. Run 25. Walk 5.	Walk 15.	Walk 5 min. Run 25. Walk 5.	Walk 15.	Walk 5 min. Run 25. Walk 5.	Walk 15 min.	Rest!
12	Walk 5 min. Run 30. Walk 5.	Walk 15.	Walk 5 min. Run 30. Walk 5.	Walk 15.	Walk 5 min. Run 30. Walk 5.	Walk 15 min.	Rest!

Source: *Run Your Way to Fitness*, American Running and Fitness Association.

Training programs for intermediate runners are also available in *The Runner's Handbook* by Bob Glover, many other running books, and on the Internet.

A fourth factor, called "specificity," also plays an important role in your progress as a runner. To improve in any sport you must develop those "specific" muscles and skills that apply to that activity. In other words, to be a better runner you have to run. To run long distances you must do some long-distance training. To run fast you must practice running fast.

Beginners are in a very tenuous position. They must run a fine line between "just enough" to improve and "not too much" to overdo. Running too often (F), too fast (I), or too long (T) can be too much for any runner's body to handle. Again, when this happens the body breaks down rather than builds up.

To progress gradually, increase only one "overload" element—F, I, or T—at a time. When the runs start feeling really easy, increase the intensity or run a little longer but don't do both at the same time. One widely suggested standard recommends not increasing mileage by more than 10 percent a week or 20 percent every two weeks.

Listen to Your Body

It helps to listen to your body. As a novice, you may not know what it's saying, but listen nonetheless. If you think you need to slow down or take a couple of days off, you probably do.

Taking Time Off

If you take off more than a week or two from running, either by choice (vacation) or by necessity (injury), build back your mileage slowly. According to Dr. Brian Sharkey in *Physiology of Fitness*, with complete bed rest fitness can decline at a rate of almost 10 percent a week. By remaining active on some level, fitness declines can be minimized.

"WALK" IS NOT A FOUR-LETTER WORD

There was a time when "walk" was indeed a four-letter word among many runners. Today that's no longer true. Former Olympian Jeff Galloway usually gets the credit for breathing life into the concept of using walks to run. For years, the first-time marathoners in his national training program have been "required" to walk one minute every three to five minutes throughout their long training runs and the marathon itself until mile eighteen.

Long-distance runner Tom Osler endorsed walking breaks even before Galloway. In his *Serious Runner's Handbook*, published in 1978, the benefits of mixing running and walking are discussed at length. Osler also shares an important lesson from his first twenty-four-hour run. "I am now convinced that the human body was not designed for long, continuous running even at a slow pace," he says. "Man can cover great distances in reasonably fast time without undue fatigue if he walks the entire way or mixes running with walking."

Walking received a tremendous credibility boost when *Runner's World* editor Amby Burfoot, a former winner of the Boston Marathon, shared "a little secret" with his nearly half million readers. "I often take walking breaks during my daily runs," he wrote in an April 1998 article, "The Run/Walk Plan." Noting the Galloway program made him a convert, Burfoot has now run four marathons with walking breaks and finished in times ranging from 3:45 to 4:30.

You don't need to be a long distance runner to benefit from walking. Beginning runners, in particular, will find that running is easier and more enjoyable if they insert walking breaks systematically into runs. To get the full benefit of the walk breaks, insert them from the beginning of the run; don't wait until you're forced by fatigue to walk. If new to fitness or returning to running after an extended absence, you may

(Continued)

even want to start by inserting running breaks into walks. As your fitness improves, gradually shorten the walks and lengthen the runs.

Run/walk training, Burfoot explains, offers many physical and mental benefits "all guaranteed to change (and probably improve) your running." Some of the benefits include increased variety, better speedwork, fewer injuries, more sightseeing, more effective recovery days, faster comebacks, and running farther, easier.

When you return to running after an extended absence, allow two days of recovery for every day off to return to your pre-hiatus level of running.

RESOURCES

For more information on beginning and fitness running read:

Brown, Richard L. and Joe Henderson. *Fitness Running.* Champaign, Ill.: Human Kinetics, 1994.

Glover, Bob, Jack Shepherd, and Shelly-lynn Florence Glover. *The Runner's Handbook.* New York: Penguin Books, 1996.

Hanc, John. *The Essential Runner.* New York: Lyons & Burford, 1994.

Higdon, Hal. *Hal Higdon's Beginning Runner's Guide.* Michigan City, Ind.: Roadrunner Press, 1997.

Joyner, "Flo-Jo" Griffith and John Hanc. *Running for Dummies.* Foster City, Calif.: IDG Books, 1999.

Rodgers, Bill with Scott Douglas. *Bill Rodgers' Lifetime Running Plan.* New York: HarperCollins, 1996.

———. *The Complete Idiot's Guide to Jogging and Running.* New York: Alpha Books, 1998.

For on-line information of specific interest to new runners go to Runner's World Online: www.newrunner.com.

For a copy of *Women's Running: The First Step,* a fifteen-page booklet for beginning runners, send a two dollar check to:

Road Runners Club of America
1150 S. Washington St., #250
Alexandria, VA 22314

CHAPTER FOUR

Getting Out the Door and Down the Road

There aren't many sports you can begin the minute you step out the door. Running is the ultimate for convenience. Many runners drive to a running destination so they can run in the woods, on a track, or with a training partner, but that's usually a choice, not a necessity. Runners rarely have trouble finding places to run. The bigger challenge is finding the time to run on a regular basis.

MAKING RUNNING A PRIORITY

In our busy lives, finding time to do any type of exercise is often difficult. We think there are more important things to do—job, family responsibilities, household chores. But you and your health deserve to be at the top of the TO DO list. And, if you put yourself there, all the other important tasks will be easier to manage. The time you spend running and exercising will be returned to you in the form of increased energy, sounder sleep, reduced stress, improved concentration, and other benefits.

Most of us can find at least thirty minutes several days a week for running. Here are a few tips to help you find the time and make running a priority.

1. *Schedule shorter, faster runs* when time is tight. By increasing the intensity of the run when you must decrease the time, you can achieve the same training benefit. Don't forget, however, that a brief warm-up and cool-down are still necessary.

2. *Plan runs when disruptions are unlikely.* If prelunch meetings cut into a scheduled lunch-hour run three days out of four, rethink your running schedule.

3. *Find a running partner.* Sometimes the issue of time is really more about motivation. Making plans to run with a friend at a specific time will help you stay committed to running.

4. *Pick a time that fits* with your internal clock. If you drag yourself out of bed every morning and barely catch the bus, don't try to be a morning runner. In all likelihood, your body wouldn't like it anyway. Find a better time when you won't compete with your body's natural desires.

5. *Piggyback your run* with another must-do activity. By looking closely at your life, you may be able to identify other time-consuming activities that are compatible with running. When it's your turn to shuttle the kids to and from soccer practice, why not suit up in running clothes? Rather than chatting on the sidelines with the other parents, go for a run or practice some form drills.

WHEN AND WHERE TO RUN

Two of the best aspects of running are its convenience and accessibility. You can take it with you and do it almost anytime and anywhere—in the city, in the country, on or off the roads, at the track, or on a treadmill. Where you run is largely a matter of personal preference and how much time is available for traveling to and from your running destination. Each running locale comes with its own unique qualities, some good and some bad.

Personal Safety

For many women (and some men), safety is a primary consideration in deciding when and where to run. According to national crime estimates, every six minutes a woman is attacked in this country. Fortunately, running is basically a very safe sport.

Don't let fear keep you from enjoying the pleasures of running outdoors; make it your ally. By taking a few simple precautions and learning basic self-defense principles, you can reduce the risk of becoming a victim.

"Verbalizing is an important self-defense technique," says Theresa Lewallan, who teaches safety to runners through the Road Runners Club of America (RRCA) AWARE=Safety workshops.

That verbalization should be in the form of yelling, not screaming. In addition to helping you breathe, yelling will allow you to tell your attacker to stop in a loud and powerful way and draw attention to what's happening.

Although there is no one pat answer for what to say and do in any given situation, Lewallan says, "Don't be afraid to embarrass yourself. Your goal is to get out alive."

Do whatever is appropriate in the situation at the time, adds AWARE instructor Jackie Burks, a sergeant with the U.S. Park Police. "The Lone Ranger is retired. Don't expect someone to rescue you."

An RRCA handout on running safety also offers these tips:

1. *Carry identification* or write your name, phone number, and blood type on the inside sole of your running shoe. Include any medical information. Don't wear jewelry.

2. *Carry coins* for a phone call.

3. *Run* with a partner.

4. *Write down or leave word* of the direction of your run. Tell friends and family your favorite running routes.

5. *Run in familiar areas.* In unfamiliar places, contact a local RRCA club or running store. Know where telephones are, or open businesses or stores. Alter your route.

6. *Always stay alert.* The more aware you are, the less vulnerable you are.

7. *Avoid unpopulated areas,* deserted streets, and overgrown trails. Especially avoid unlit areas at night. Run clear of parked cars or bushes.

8. *Don't wear headsets.* Use your ears to be aware of your surroundings.

9. *Ignore verbal harassment.* Use discretion in acknowledging strangers. Look directly at others and be observant, but keep your distance and keep moving.

10. *Run against traffic* so you can observe approaching automobiles.

11. *Wear reflective material* if you must run before dawn or after dark.

12. *Use your intuition* about a person or an area. React on your intuitions and avoid the person or place if you're unsure.

13. *Practice memorizing* license tags or identifying characteristics of strangers.

14. *Carry a whistle* or other noisemaker.

15. *CALL POLICE IMMEDIATELY* if something happens to you or someone else or you notice anyone out of the ordinary.

RUNNING ON THE ROAD

A large percentage of runners use the roads in and around their communities because they're easy and convenient. Considered pedestrians, runners are expected to follow basic rules of the road. Run single file and stay alert to vehicles and bicycles. To reduce the risk of traffic-related accidents, always run on the sidewalk, face traffic, obey traffic laws or signals, and cross streets at corners. If no sidewalks are provided, face traffic and move to the shoulder as far from the road as practical. By seeing vehicles as they approach, you can brace yourself for those strong gusts of wind and be better prepared to alert a driver of your intentions or dodge an errant vehicle.

Dawn and dusk are especially dangerous times for road runners. The glare of the rising and setting sun on shiny hoods and windows can be particularly blinding to drivers. Try to avoid running near cars when the sun is low in the sky and shining into the eyes of drivers.

The dark of night and early morning can also present hazards. If you are going to run in the dark, make yourself visible. Always wear white or a light-colored top and add a reflective vest and light. Most running stores carry these items plus a variety of garments with illuminating features. The blinking lights or reflective patches offered on some shoes are a nice touch but you need to be more visible in the dark. It is always a good practice to run defensively, but even more so at night or during inclement weather. Assume that cars cannot see you and act accordingly.

RUNNING IN CIRCLES

One of the real joys of running on a track is the absence of traditional road hazards like vehicles and dogs. Tracks offer much softer surfaces than the cement or asphalt found on roadways, plus it's easier to obtain accurate measurements of your pace and workout mileage. One lap around most outdoor tracks is 400 meters, about one-quarter mile. Some tracks are dirt while many new ones are made of shock-absorbing synthetic materials.

The major downside of track running is the monotony and boredom that set in after a few minutes of running around in circles. Indoor tracks, which tend to be shorter and require more turns, can also be a source of injury to the inside leg if you run a lot of laps without reversing directions.

The outdoor tracks found at most high schools and colleges are usually open to the public when not in use for team training. Open hours may be posted at the facility, or a quick call to the athletic department will confirm the track's availability.

Standard track etiquette dictates that runners move counterclockwise around a track and that slower runners use the lanes to the outside. Always yield to faster runners by moving to the right, not the left. If you want to change directions to balance the potential risks of always turning the same way, run clockwise in an outside lane when the track isn't busy.

RUNNING WILD

Many runners never venture far from the security of the track or paved roads close to home. But those who do have discovered that running trails in parks and wilderness areas offer an unparalleled experience. The additional challenges presented by unstable footing, poorly marked trails, elevation changes, and potential perils (from tiny ticks to mighty mountain lions), are balanced by beauty and quiet rarely found on the road.

Trail running isn't for everyone. If you hate dirty shoes, are prone to ankle injuries, have no sense of direction, or expect basic necessities like drinking fountains and bathrooms, you probably should stay closer to home.

According to ultrarunner Tom Morstein-Marx, trail running is similar to fast hiking. As such, he says, "all the basic rules of the outdoors apply." Carry fluids, be prepared for things like poison oak, watch for changes in the weather, and tell someone where you are running.

Of course, the extent of your preparations will depend on the location of the trail. Running with a group of friends on an urban trail in New York's Central Park or San Francisco's Golden Gate Park is very different from running alone in the wilderness many miles from civilization.

RUNNING NOWHERE

Treadmills, currently the best-selling piece of aerobic equipment for the home exerciser, provide one of the most convenient and flexible ways to run without worrying about issues like the weather and safety.

Treadmills offer variable speeds and grades for all levels of running ability. The decks of many models also absorb much more impact than outdoor surfaces. Like running on a track, some people find treadmills boring. To fight the monotony of running nowhere fast, put on headphones or watch television. Some runners even place their treadmills by the window to feel like they're running outdoors.

According to the Sporting Goods Manufacturers Association's annual survey of fitness trends, treadmill use increased 720 percent from 1987 to 1997. This trend is expected to continue.

IN THE MARKET FOR A TREADMILL?

If you're planning to purchase a treadmill, put on running shoes and give several prospective models a test run. Be sure to consider these factors:

- Is it constructed and designed to handle your weight and size?
- Does it remain stable at various speeds and inclines?
- Is it quiet enough for your comfort?
- Does the deck absorb enough impact to meet your needs?
- Are the controls easy to use?
- Does it offer features you want (i.e., preprogrammed workouts, heart-rate monitoring, fitness testing, emergency stop button)?
- Does it come with care and maintenance instructions?
- Is a warranty offered and adequate?
- Do you have room for a space-consuming piece of equipment?
- Will you really use it?

If you are new to treadmills, the first few runs will feel awkward—like trying to walk on a swinging bridge. It gets easier with practice, but don't look down; you may get dizzy.

For safety's sake, never stand on the belt when turning a treadmill on or off. It may send you flying. Instead, grab ahold of the console or frame and straddle the belt, then flip the switch. After adjusting the speed to slow, step on and start walking. Gradually increase the speed and elevation until you are running at the desired intensity. You shouldn't need to hold on to maintain speed or balance during a workout. At the end of a workout, slowly decrease the speed to cool-down, then grab the console and straddle the belt before switching off the treadmill. Be sure the belt stops and you have your "land" legs back before stepping to the ground.

Although treadmills offer similar aerobic benefits to running on the road, the two activities are not entirely comparable. To compensate for the lack of wind resistance and the ease of foot turnover on a moving belt, add 0.5 to 1 percent grade. With this adjustment, the effort required to run on a treadmill will be fairly equal to the road. If you intend to enter a road race, spend some time pounding the pavement beforehand or your body may not be happy on race day.

DOGS: BEST FRIENDS AND FOES

To a runner, dogs can be both friend and foe. A well-trained pet that is built and conditioned to run can provide miles of faithful companionship and security. On the other hand, an unrestrained or out-of-control animal can take the fun out of your run, if you, your dog, or someone else gets hurt.

Running with the Dogs

If you run enough miles, you are bound to encounter a wayward dog that acts as if you're its next meal. The barks of most dogs are indeed worse than their bites. Their menacing manner is usually just a way to inform you that you're in their territory. Some runners, like mail carriers, carry small canisters of dog repellant. The dog must be within about ten feet for any spray to be effective.

What you do will depend on the size of the dog, how close it is, and how much time you have to respond to a potential threat.

Often a commanding "Go Home!" or "Bad Dog!" is enough to send the animal on its way. Some dogs will lose interest if you stand still, then slowly walk away. If you try to run, chase is likely to ensue.

Running with Your Own Dog

If you are thinking about taking your pet out for a run, marathon runner and veterinarian Noel Dybdal suggests you consider these points:

- Is the dog trained to run on a leash and obey your commands?
- Is the dog conditioned for the planned distance or duration?
- Is the weather, location, and running surface appropriate for your pet?
- Will adequate water be available before, during, and after the run?

If you can answer these questions affirmatively, Dybdal says, you may have found a very reliable running partner. Keep in mind, however, that animals are a lot like people. Before starting a new exercise program, your pet should be examined by a veterinarian to make sure the animal doesn't have physical problems that prevent healthy running or need to be addressed.

Build your dog's mileage gradually, Dybdal notes. One or two miles is often plenty for a puppy or smaller dog, while larger, mature dogs can be conditioned to go much farther. Your running pace should allow the dog to trot along comfortably at your side. When letting a dog lead, many runners have a tendency to lean forward from the hips. This body position puts pressure on the lower back and should be avoided to reduce the risk of injury. (See chapter five for more information on running form.)

> **WHICH BREEDS MAKE THE BEST RUNNERS?**
>
> Generally, the best dogs for running are larger dogs with long legs such as Dobermans, Rhodesian ridgebacks, German shepherds, and point setters. A large dog can be conditioned to run many miles. Smaller dogs under thirty pounds, such as Australian shepherds, should run no more than an hour.
>
> Be especially cautious with golden retrievers, Labradors, rottweilers, and other breeds that are prone to hip dysplasia and elbow problems.

The ideal training distance and pace for your dog will vary according to its age, breed, and conditioning. Your veterinarian can help determine how much running your dog can handle.

During a run, be especially alert to the dog's attitude and the condition of its paws. We have shoes to protect our feet from hot, hard surfaces but a dog doesn't. If your dog is used to running on grass, for example, don't spend more than fifteen minutes at one time on pavement until its paws are toughened.

While you can recognize your own fatigue, body-temperature changes, and need for water, dogs can't talk. They like to run; don't assume your dog will stop when it gets tired. Dehydration and overheating may not be evident until the situation is severe. When offering water to your dog during or after a run, give only small amounts at first, then allow the animal to quench its thirst. If you suspect heatstroke, move the animal immediately to a shady area and sponge it off with water.

There are several warning signs that may indicate your pet is experiencing serious fatigue, dehydration, or injury:

- Rapid breathing
- Loud panting
- Ears pulled back

- Reluctance to run, or stopping during a run
- Staggering, altered gait, or lameness

Responsibilities That Come with Your Dog

The joys of running with a dog also come with some responsibilities. Always use a leash if the law requires it or if other people or animals are in the area. Remember, not everyone may share your enthusiasm for running dogs. Also, honor any prohibitions against pets established by race or running-club officials, who must make people's safety a priority. Also, carry a plastic bag and clean up after your pet. No one likes the smell of dog poop and it's hard to remove from running-shoe treads.

RESOURCES

To request a map of running routes in a specific U.S. city, contact the American Running and Fitness Association (ARFA). Use of the ARFA running trails network, which includes maps for hundreds of cities, is a free service for association members. Nonmembers pay a small fee or can receive a free map by providing a new map in exchange.

American Running and Fitness Association
4405 East West Hwy., Suite 405
Bethesda, MD 20814
Phone: 1-800-776-ARFA
Fax: (301) 913-9520
E-mail: arfarun@aol.com
Web site: www.arfa.org

For good places to run here and abroad, go to Run the Planet at www.runtheplanet.com. Add your favorite local routes so that others can enjoy them while visiting your city.

For more information on trail running:

All American Trail Running Association
PO Box 9175
Colorado Springs, CO 80932
Phone: (719) 633-9740
E-mail: trlrunner@aol.com
Web site: www.trailrunner.com

CHAPTER FIVE

Picking Up the Pace and Running in the Fast Lane

Being able to run faster with less effort is one of those eventualities that happens to new runners as their bodies adapt to the stress of running. Unfortunately, after a year or two of consistent running you won't get much faster unless you work out and train with speed in mind. To improve, you must do speedwork and adopt a number of additional training principles.

For many runners, picking up the pace and running faster is a challenge and a goal. Some want speed to be competitive in their age groups at races while others want just enough speed so they don't come in last. Fitness runners who don't race at all like to get faster because it's a tangible way to measure improvement.

SETTING GOALS

According to experts, goal-setting is an important step in improving any fitness program (or other matters in your life). Goals will give your training purpose, help keep you motivated, and provide a way to measure progress.

Before reading any further, take a moment to write a preliminary running or fitness goal in the space below or on a separate piece of paper. Think about your goal in terms of where you are today and where you want to be next month, next year, or next decade. Don't worry about setting your goal in stone. You can always refine it or rewrite a different goal later.

_____

_____

_____

Runner Jeanette Link, an exercise physiologist and certified personal trainer, always encourages her clients to set goals, make them "SMART," and write them down. A SMART goal, she says, is:

- Simple and specific
- Measurable
- Action-oriented
- Realistic
- Timely

According to Link, a goal such as "to run faster" is too general and vague to put into practice. A goal should be specific and include an action plan. "It's nice to have goals but you need a plan to get you there," she says. "You can set yourself up for success by incorporating a plan of action into your goals."

To make your goal realistic, Link suggests breaking down the ultimate goal into smaller, manageable steps. You may actually need three goals: a short-term, intermediate, and final goal. Additionally, Link notes that a goal should include a time element and be measurable to evaluate success.

If you currently run a 4:30 marathon and your goal is four hours and qualifying for the Boston Marathon by the end of the year, you may need to establish several interim mileage or pace goals to stay motivated month after month. You may also need to ask yourself if Boston is a realistic goal given the time you have to devote to running. A realistic goal for a beginning runner might be to run a certain distance by a specific date.

Be conservative in setting goals. You can always make another goal after reaching the first one. Taking lots of baby steps and being successful is a lot more rewarding than risking a fall from one giant leap gone awry.

Now, go back to the goal you drafted earlier and see if it is specific and simple, measurable, action-oriented, realistic, and timely. Here's an example of how an original goal was rewritten using the SMART system.

Original goal: To run faster.

SMART goal: To cut one minute off my 10-K time at the Peachtree Road Race by adding one interval session a week to my current training for the next eight weeks.

Take a few minutes to rewrite your SMART goal in the space provided below or on a separate piece of paper.

_____

_____

_____

Finally, recognize that your initial enthusiasm for achieving a goal won't always remain the same. Try setting up a fitness-appropriate reward system such as buying a new running accessory or book when you achieve each short-term or interim goal. It is also useful to write your goals down and share them with others to become truly committed.

"By writing your goals down it's more real," Link says. "Over time you can look back and see progress." At the end of the first week or month you can then evaluate your success and revise the action plan and goal accordingly.

KEEPING A RECORD OF YOUR RUNNING

Whether you write goals or not, having some type of record—a log, a diary, or a calendar with notes—of your running will be extremely beneficial in evaluating your training program and progress (or lack thereof) as a runner.

The actual format of running records is less important than the content and the need to record information on a regular basis. Try to find a record-keeping system that fits your needs and desires.

In the introductory pages of his new training journal, Jeff Galloway suggests that runners use a journal to "write your own book about fitness and running." By recording the experiences and data that are important to you, he says, "you can bring visions into reality. By interacting with these journal pages, you'll chart out your own journey, which will bestow a great deal of confidence in your mission."

Many runners start out with a simple running diary or calendar and then switch to a more elaborate logging system as they recognize the value of having more data to analyze.

If a computer is essentially an extension of your fingertips for most of the day, a training-log software may be the most convenient format. There are literally dozens of computer logs on the market and many offer free trial disks and coaching components for planning your training. (See the appendix for software listings.)

For paper-and-pencil people, a commercial running logbook or journal will work well. Some of the most popular ones also include running tips and training information. People who like to keep things simple may choose to scribble running notes in their daily planners or calendars.

What should you include in your record-keeping? Generally, the more information you record, the more useful it will be in the future. The basic information should include specific workout data (date, type of workout, distance, time, intensity, heart rate). You may also want to include conditions affecting your workout (weather, terrain, amount of sleep), personal information (weight, resting heart rate, mood, diet), and special information (race results, injuries, changes in shoes, goals).

This sample log page from *The Triathlon Log* by Sally Edwards provides space to record data for three different activities. Copy this page for personal use or purchase a logbook from a running specialty store.

DATE	SPORT	DISTANCE	TIME	TYPE WKOUT	PULSE	HRS. SLEEP WEIGHT MOOD	COMMENTS
M						HRS / LBS / 🙂🙂🙂	
T						HRS / LBS / 🙂🙂🙂	
W						HRS / LBS / 🙂🙂🙂	
T						HRS / LBS / 🙂🙂🙂	
F						HRS / LBS / 🙂🙂🙂	
S						HRS / LBS / 🙂🙂🙂	
S						HRS / LBS / 🙂🙂🙂	

	SWIM	BICYCLE	RUN	COMMENTS:
Total Distance For Week				
Total Training Hrs.				
Distance Year To Date				

WEEK #

TRAINING TO IMPROVE

The principles of training and racing have evolved over many years and continue to change as coaches, athletes, doctors, and scientists learn more about how the body functions and adapts to repeated cycles of physiological stress and recovery.

Although training must be specific and individualized to be effective, most running programs incorporate a few basic concepts to build endurance, strength, and speed. Keep in mind that training is different from simply exercising or going out for a run. It's a systematic, planned approach to achieving a specific goal.

Training to Build Base

The first phase of any training program is known as "building base." That is the most important stage of training because it becomes the foundation for all later stages. It is a time of easy, comfortable, aerobic running several times a week to increase endurance and stamina.

At the same time that the entire cardiovascular system is learning to function more efficiently, your muscles are training to handle the demands of running and resisting fatigue. For beginning runners, all workouts are essentially devoted to building a base. Don't ever feel the need to rush this stage because a solid foundation will eventually make the faster, harder running much easier.

Using the Long Run to Build Endurance

The long run is a key component for building and maintaining a running base. The easiest way to get faster without training faster is to extend an average-length run into a longer run. The purpose of the long run is to build endurance so that shorter distances feel easier.

This type of training, also known as "long slow distance," has been a staple element in training programs for several decades. Joe

Henderson wrote about it thirty years ago in the booklet *LSD: The Humane Way to Train.*

Depending on its length, the long run should be done at least once a month but no more than once a week. To get the most benefit, the long run must be done at a slow, comfortable pace.

The length of each person's long run will vary according to their goals and the length of their normal run or race distance. Jeff Galloway makes the following recommendations:

Race Distance	Long Run
5-K	12 miles
10-K	15–17 miles
Half Marathon	20 miles
Marathon	28–30 miles

To reach the desired long-run distance without risking injury, increase the mileage gradually and run at least one to two minutes per mile slower than you could do the distance on that day. As Galloway stresses in his book, *Marathon,* "the slower you go, the faster you'll recover."

To lengthen the long run, he says, start with the distance of your longest run in the last two weeks and add one mile every week until it reaches twelve miles. After twelve miles, add two miles to the long run every other week. At eighteen miles, add up to three miles every third week. During the alternating weeks, Galloway suggests doing a shorter long run, equal to half the distance of the longest run so far but not more than ten miles.

Hill Training to Get Stronger

Once a runner has developed adequate endurance to run a desired distance, hillwork can be introduced in a training schedule to build leg strength. Running hills, doing hill repeats, and climbing stairs are basic forms of strength training which use body weight for the resistance. Strength training is important because it makes subsequent speed workouts easier. Hillwork also introduces the body to more strenuous running.

When running hills, keep your feet low to the ground, maintain a quick turnover, and shorten your stride slightly until the hamstrings (muscles on the back of the thigh) relax. Your body position should be perpendicular to the horizontal, not the incline of the hill.

Don't make the mistake of thinking you need big, long hills for hillwork. A hill that is a few hundred yards long with a grade of less than 5 percent is plenty for most runners in the beginning. Start with two or three hills and build to a maximum of eight to ten hills. If you can't maintain good form as described here and later in this chapter, the hill is too steep.

Speed Training to Run Faster

There are many different forms of speed training and all serve the same purpose—teaching the body to run fast both physiologically and biomechanically. Speed training is a process that requires you to run anaerobically (without enough oxygen) and experience a buildup of lactic acid or lactate, a by-product of the energy process. Concentrations of lactate in the muscles and blood, and unmet demands for oxygen (oxygen debt), are primary causes of fatigue. As the body adapts to speed training, its aerobic capacity (also known as $VO_{2\ MAX}$) and lactate tolerance (threshold) improve. You can run faster, longer, and easier.

Three of the most common types of speedwork include fartlek, tempo runs, and intervals. *Fartlek* is the Swedish word for "speed play." It's a playful, totally free-form run that includes a few seconds or minutes of fast running inserted randomly throughout a run. After warming up, for example, you accelerate to the first street sign. Then after running slowly to get your wind back, accelerate to the red car. The entire run, or fartlek, is a series of short, sporadic speed bursts alternating with easy running. This type of speed training is a fun and easy remedy for "one-paceitis," a tongue-in-cheek condition many recreational runners have and don't want.

Tempo runs. Used to help maintain long, hard running. They force you to train steadily at about racing pace but for a shorter period of time. Usually twenty to forty minutes in length, excluding a 1-to-2-mile warm-up and a short cool-down, tempo runs feel hard but doable.

For those who race, the tempo-run pace should be about fifteen to twenty seconds per mile slower than 10-K pace or thirty seconds slower than 5-K pace. If you train at this "tempo," you are teaching the body to better handle the effects of hard running, such as the accumulation of lactate. When tempo runs are done at a constant, steady state for an accurately measured distance (like a track), they can also teach you to run at an even pace.

Interval training. This is one of the most common forms of speedwork. Typically performed on a track, it is characterized by repeated periods of high-speed running, followed by periods of recovery. The terminology for interval training is often confusing. Repeated intervals of the same distance are referred to as repetitions, reps, or repeats. A series of reps is called a set. The period between each interval is a recovery, which allows for rest and recuperation.

The race distance you're training for determines the pace, the number of and length of reps, and the duration of the recovery interval (work-to-rest ratio). Generally, reps are longer, slower, and less numerous for longer races.

Nearly all runners want to be faster and many make the mistake of doing speedwork without having an adequate base or the strength to support it. Instead of getting faster, they get injured, discouraged, or fatigued, or experience symptoms of overtraining. Structured speedwork, like interval training, isn't usually recommended until you've been running consistently (thirty-minute runs, at least three days a week) for six months to a year.

Hard/Easy Training to Run Better

Even the world's best runners don't run hard and fast all the time and neither should you. Anytime you run harder and faster than normal, give your body time to recover. It needs a minimum of forty-eight hours to renew the energy stores that fuel the muscles. To get a lot faster and stronger hard runs are essential, but so are the easy days that should follow.

Rest and Recovery to Rejuvenate

It may seem unusual to include rest as a training principle but without it the strenuous part can be rendered worthless. As discussed earlier, running improvement occurs through repeated cycles of progressive overload. The body will only become stronger if it is given an opportunity to rest and recover after being stressed. Remember, training is stress—stressing the body to run longer, harder, more often, and under different conditions. Inadequate recovery leads to injury and overtraining, neither of which makes you fitter, faster, or stronger. (Injuries and overtraining are discussed in chapter seven.)

MIND GAMES

Many men and women are born with the genetic makeup and physical traits to become talented athletes. Some excel by virtue of natural talent and others benefit from the tutelage of knowledgeable coaches. Only a handful of the physically talented athletes ever join the ranks of "great" athletes. Those who do have what it takes both physically and mentally to be the best in their sports. The mental techniques and skills of top athletes are the same ones you can use to run your best.

Right-Brain Running

In 1979, art professor Betty Edwards wrote the book *Drawing on the Right Side of the Brain*. She applied the discoveries of brain research and the dual nature of human thinking (verbal and analytical thinking mainly in the left hemisphere, and visual and perceptual thinking mainly in the right hemisphere) to the teaching of drawing skills.

In his marathon training programs throughout the country, Jeff Galloway teaches how to run on the right side of the brain. His strategy is to give the verbal, analytical left brain a job it doesn't want to do so that the right brain can take over. In running (and life), the left brain, Galloway says, has a million logical reasons why you can't do something. "It tries to protect you and usually it is overprotective." The right side won't try to argue with the left. Instead, it will create imaginative ways to move you in the direction of your abilities.

The right brain is intuitive and unlikely to lead you into dangerous situations. To help your right brain in its efforts, relax, take the pressure off yourself, and focus on the positive. You can also engage the right brain by telling a joke, laughing, or thinking about something silly like wearing two left shoes. "If you decrease the anticipated stress, you lower the left brain's control," Galloway explains.

Mental Imaging and Visualization

Visualization, also called imagery or imagining, is a technique in which the runner or athlete creates a mental picture and feeling of how they want to perform. Rather than telling yourself to relax, create a positive mental image of a relaxed runner. While watching that picture in the mind's eye, try to create the feelings of running relaxed and strong.

It isn't clear how visualization works but one theory suggests the brain can't distinguish between similar actions that are imagined or actually happen. By mentally rehearsing a desired action over and over, it becomes easier to perform because you have a memory of it.

For the most effective visualization, draw on all your senses, not just the visual images. Explore every detail—the sounds, the smells, the feelings—and add them to your mental image. Like running, you must practice visualization regularly to get the optimum benefits.

In her book, *Running for Dummies,* the late Florence "Flo-Jo" Griffith Joyner recommends runners practice visualization everyday. "It complements your physical training and will help you reach your goals."

"Magic" Words and Self-Talk

Attaching cue words to mental images and desired behaviors is another powerful mental tool. In the 1983 movie *On the Edge,* runner Wes Holman, played by actor Bruce Dern, trains endless hours in the hills preparing for a comeback. He uses two words: "soar" when burning up the hills and "burn" when soaring down the hills.

Galloway marathoners, who run in groups of seven to ten, actually have three "magic" words printed on the backs of their shirts. During training and the marathon itself, they see and use the words "relax," "power," and "glide" to recall the feelings and behaviors they want to perform.

To use mental training, choose cue words, positive statements, and mental images that are meaningful to you.

RUNNING IN GOOD FORM

There are several schools of thought on running form. Some coaches and athletes believe your form is your form and it shouldn't be changed for any reason. Others believe that only injury-related form deficiencies should be changed. The most moderate perspective encourages runners to learn and practice the basics of good running form.

Most recreational runners and a lot of competitors never have an opportunity to learn about good running form. Instead of running the way their bodies want to perform naturally, they try to emulate the runners they see and admire. Most of the best runners adopt a form that compensates for their own individual anatomy and body structure. Their successes are based more on training and genetics than good technique and efficiency. Try to think of the ideal form rather than emulating another runner.

New runners don't need to worry about form; beginners primarily should get used to the basic mechanics of running. As fitness and strength improve, running will become more efficient and easier.

Whether you run for fitness or competition, good running form can:

1. *Improve efficiency*—you'll run faster with less effort.

2. *Reduce the likelihood* of form-related injuries.

3. *Make you feel good* so running is more enjoyable.

The elements of good form are basically the same for all running events except for the increased arm action and foot strike of short sprint distances. For any distance longer than 5,000 meters (5-K), keep the following techniques in mind:

Overall body position. Maintain a vertical body position; do not lean forward. Keep your head over the shoulders and shoulders over the hips. If you have lower-back pain during a run you're probably leaning or arching the lower back. The easiest way to correct your alignment is to keep the hips tucked under and "run tall."

Head and neck. The position of the head is often dictated by what the eyes are doing. To keep your head level, don't look at the ground in front of your feet. Watch for obstacles in your path without lowering your head by looking out a few yards in front.

If your neck muscles are frequently sore during or after a run, you may be lifting your chin and tilting the head back. Large-breasted women sometimes do this to compensate for the extra weight in front. Stay relaxed and pay attention to body alignment—head, shoulders, and hips.

Shoulders and arms. The primary function of the shoulders and arms at slow and moderate speeds is balance. At higher speeds and on hills they can also provide extra propulsion. Keep the entire upper body relaxed. The arm swing should be a forward and back motion. Letting them sway side to side or across the midline of the chest will reduce efficiency. The wrists should remain loose and the hands can be cupped but not clenched.

Legs and feet. If your body alignment is vertical and the hips are tucked under, there's not much else for the legs to do except run. The most common lower body mistakes include overstriding (lengthening the stride so the foot lands in front of the knee), lifting the knees too high in front, and kicking the heels too high in the rear.

Do not try to lengthen your stride or lift your knees and heels in an attempt to run faster. The key to running efficiently is faster turnover, or quicker steps, not necessarily longer strides. Your body will find the stride length that's natural for you. The correct stride will put the landing foot under your center of gravity. By keeping the feet close to the ground, a quick turnover is easier. Quick turnover also limits vertical bounce because the need to remain airborne is reduced. Keep the motion going forward, not up and down or side to side.

Whether your feet hit the ground heel first, toe first, or flat is largely determined by foot biomechanics, but shoes and orthotics also have an effect. A heel-to-toe motion is generally considered the most efficient and is used by most distance runners. However, "foot plant" or "foot strike" is very difficult to change and not especially critical unless it is creating problems. In the long run, the body will adapt to the foot plant that is most appropriate and the running distance.

You won't learn good running form in a week or even a month. But by taking a few minutes during each run to review your technique, efficiency will eventually become second nature.

Being videotaped from the side while running is a great way to analyze your form. The camera will capture areas for improvement that you may not be able to feel. (You can also observe your form while running past a row of store windows.) Look particularly at your trunk. Do you lean forward rather than maintain a vertical body position? Is your pelvis tucked under? Do the shoulders and arms look relaxed? Play the tape in slow motion and watch for that point in time when all of your weight is on one foot. If the foot is in front of the knee, you are overstriding. Don't try to change your running form drastically, even if it needs lots of improvement. Spend a few minutes each week and concentrate on one or two of the most significant problems.

RESOURCES

For more information on training and racing read:

Burfoot, Amby. *Runner's World Complete Book of Running: Everything You Need to Know to Run for Fun, Fitness and Competition.* Emmaus, Pa.: Rodale Press, 1997.

Galloway, Jeff. *Galloway's Book on Running.* Bolinas, Calif.: Shelter Publications, 1984.

Henderson, Joe. *Best Runs.* Champaign, Ill.: Human Kinetics, 1996.

Higdon, Hal. *Hal Higdon's Smart Running: Expert Advice on Training, Motivation, Injury Prevention, Nutrition and Good Health for Runners of any Age and Ability.* Emmaus, Pa.: Rodale Press, 1998.

————. *How to Train.* Emmaus, Pa.: Rodale Press, 1997.

Lebow, Fred and Gloria Averbuch. *The New York Road Runners Club Complete Book of Running & Fitness.* New York: Random House, 1998.

Pfitzinger, Pete and Scott Douglas. *Road Racing for Serious Runners: Training to Race 5-K Through the Marathon.* Champaign, Ill.: Human Kinetics, 1998.

Sheehan, George. *Running to Win.* Emmaus, Pa.: Rodale Press, 1992.

For information on marathon training read:

Bakoulis, Gordon Bloch. *How to Train For & Run Your Best Marathon.* New York: Simon & Schuster/Fireside Books, 1993.
Galloway, Jeff. *Marathon!* Atlanta, Ga.: Phidippides Publications, 1996.
Hanc, John. *The Essential Marathoner.* New York: Lyons and Burford, 1996.
Henderson, Joe. *Marathon Training: The Proven 100-Day Program for Success.* Champaign, Ill.: Human Kinetics, 1997.
Higdon, Hal. *Marathon.* Emmaus, Pa.: Rodale Press, 1993.
Keuhls, Dave. *4 Months to a 4-Hour Marathon.* New York: Berkeley Publishing Group, 1998.

For more comprehensive and technical running information of interest to serious athletes and coaches read:

Martin, David and Peter Coe. *Better Training for Distance Runners.* Champaign, Ill.: Human Kinetics, 1997.
Newsholme, Eric, Tony Leech, and Glenda Duester. *The Science of Training and Performance.* England: John Wiley & Sons, 1994.
Noakes, Timothy. *Lore of Running.* Champaign, Ill.: Leisure Press, 1991.

For more information on mental training read:

Lynch, Jerry and Warren Scott. *Running Within: A Guide to Mastering the Body-Mind-Spirit Connection for Ultimate Training and Racing.* Champaign, Ill.: Human Kinetics, 1999.
Ungerleider, Steven. *Mental Training for Peak Performance.* Emmaus, Pa.: Rodale Press, 1996.

On-line training schedules for specific races and/or distances can be found at:

Avon: www.avonrunning.com
Coaching Forum: www.telecall.co.uk/~pault

Hal Higdon: www.halhigdon.com
Runner's World "Training and Racing": www.runnersworld.com
Team Oregon: www.teamoregon.com

To receive a single copy of *ARFA's Guide to Running and Racing,* send a business-size, self-addressed, stamped (55¢) envelope:

American Running and Fitness Association
4405 East West Hwy., Suite 405
Bethesda, MD 20814

For free demo disks of running log/training software:

The Athlete's Diary
Steven's Creek Software
21346 Rumford Dr.
Cupertino, CA 95014
Phone: 1-800-TA-DIARY
Fax: (408) 725-0424
Web site: www.stevenscreek.com

PC Coach
Phone: 1-800-522-6224
or (303) 442-1818
Fax: (303) 494-9722
E-mail: pccoach@pccoach.com
Web site: www.pccoach.com

UltraCoach
Phone: 1-800-400-1390
Fax: (909) 625-4504
E-mail: ucinfo@ultracch.com
Web site: www.ultracch.com

A few of the popular training logs for runners include:

American Running and Fitness Association's Runners Log.
Jeff Galloway's Training Journal. Atlanta, Ga.: Phidippides Publication, 1998.
Bill Rodgers Classic Running Log. Huntington Concepts, 1991.

If you are an American post-collegiate runner who, while struggling financially, shows great promise to develop into an accomplished national and world-class athlete, you may be eligible for an RRCA Roads Scholar grant. For information or to contribute to the program:

Road Runners Club of America
1150 S. Washington St., #250
Alexandria, VA 22314
Phone: (703) 836-0558
Fax: (703) 836-4430
E-mail: office@rrca.org
Web site: www.rrca.org

CHAPTER SIX

Crossing Over to the Road Beyond Running

If you're one of those runners who scoffs at the thought of spending valuable training time on some nonrunning activity, you might want to reconsider. Your running may actually improve if supplemented with training in other aerobic and non-aerobic activities. "Cross-training," as it's termed, is especially popular with athletes who participate in high-impact sports like running.

WHY CROSS-TRAIN?

While running is truly a great form of cardiovascular exercise that strengthens the heart, lungs, and legs, it doesn't promote overall physical fitness. Over time, men and women who limit their exercise exclusively to running are more likely to develop muscle imbalances, lose upper-body strength, and decrease flexibility. The normal mechanics of running, for example, tend to develop hamstrings (muscles on the back of the thigh) and make them much stronger than the quadriceps (a group of four muscles on the front of the thigh). This imbalance can eventually lead to injury. A lack of flexibility can affect running form and prevent the body from moving fluidly through the full range of motion.

Many runners also lack upper body strength. That's no surprise to most people because only the legs get a significant amount of exercise. The arms may not seem that important during running but they provide forward momentum and balance. Just try to run a quarter mile with your arms dangling at your sides. At the end of a long race or running up a hill, a strong upper body can help you maintain your pace. Single-sport athletes are also prone to overuse injuries because the same muscle groups and joints are often stressed repeatedly without time for adequate recovery.

Although cross-training or incorporating nonrunning activities into a running program contradicts the long-held principle of "specificity" (only running makes you a good runner), many athletes, coaches, and experts now recognize that there are good reasons to complement running with other activities.

In *The Physician and Sportsmedicine*, Bryant Stamford notes that cross-training helps athletes:

- Stay interested by adding variety to workouts.
- Reduce the risk of injury by distributing the training load to various parts of the body.
- Develop the whole body, not just parts.
- Keep training healthy muscles and joints when other parts of the body are injured.

According to Gary Moran, coauthor of three books—*Getting Stronger, Dynamics of Strength Training,* and *Cross-Training for Sports*—cross-training is especially valuable to runners and other athletes because it allows them to extend training with less risk of overtraining or injury.

"Structurally we are built to handle a certain number of miles," explains Moran, who earned his doctorate in anatomy and biomechanics and later served as director of research at Nike. "For some runners that limit may only be thirty miles. For most everybody it is less than one hundred miles a week. Cross-training is a way of training beyond your running limit."

SOME ACTIVITIES ARE BETTER THAN OTHERS

In selecting any nonrunning activity for cross-training, consider your interests and objective or goals. If you are cross-training because of an injury, select a sport that provides adequate training benefits without aggravating the problem area. For a pleasant diversion from running day-in and day-out, pick an activity you enjoy. If you hope to rest your running muscles, your choices will be more limited. Some sports and activities offer more running-related benefits than others.

ENDURANCE TRAINING

In the best of all worlds, most runners would do all of their aerobic and anaerobic endurance workouts by running. Unfortunately, most of our bodies won't let us pound the pavement mile after mile. The crossover benefits of nonspecific training in specialty sports became evident during the 1980s in the early days of the triathlon, a triple-sport event involving running, cycling, and swimming. With only so many hours in a day for training, triathletes were forced to cut back on their primary sport to make time for training in the others. Many athletes found they were still able to perform well in their specialty even though multisport training required a reduction in primary-sport training. Data now supports the idea that nonspecific but muscularly similar training like stair-climbing may even contribute to enhanced running performance.

While almost any aerobic sport that is continuous in nature and uses the large muscle groups can be used by runners for effective cross-training, four sports—deep-water running, cycling, cross-country skiing, and stair-climbing—are considered among the best alternatives. Swimming can also provide benefits.

Deep-water running. A nonimpact alternative to pounding the pavement, deep-water running is an effective technique for maintaining and even improving running performance. It is primarily used for training during injuries and later-term pregnancy.

Deep-water runners usually wear a flotation device, a belt or vest which is widely available for around $50, to stay afloat while simulating running in place on land. To get the most benefits from this form of cross-training, pay attention to your in-water form.

The body, most experts say, should remain in an upright position while the legs duplicate a running (not bicycling) motion. A normal running arm swing (not the dog paddle) should also be used. Don't worry about propelling yourself around the pool, it's the water's resistance that gives the muscles a workout. Also, lower your training heart rate by about ten beats per minute to allow for the effects of the water. Most regular land workouts like interval training and tempo runs can easily be duplicated in the water.

Cycling. A popular cross-training choice of runners because it develops different leg muscles, cycling offers similar aerobic benefits. Cycling, Moran says, is also an excellent warm-up and cooldown for running. Before running, he says, cycling increases blood flow to the muscles by opening the capillary beds. After running, it flushes out lactic acid and other metabolic wastes to speed recovery.

Although outdoor cycling can be more enjoyable than indoor stationary cycling, traffic and road hazards sometimes limit the ability to train continuously at aerobic levels comparable to running. For endurance, try to maintain a high pedal speed or cadence (revolutions per minute or rpm). Pedaling at around 80 rpm's will help enhance leg speed.

Mile for mile and minute for minute, running and cycling are not equal. You will usually have to cycle longer to obtain benefits similar to running. Some triathletes estimate that two minutes of cycling is about the same as one minute of running at similar levels of effort. If you intend to use a heart-rate monitor for cycling, adjust the training zones to that sport. Maximum heart rates for cycling are usually seven to ten beats per minute lower than for running due to less arm use.

Before heading out for a ride or climbing on a stationary cycle, make sure the bike fits you. Adjust the seat so that the leg is nearly straight when your foot is at the lowest point. The handlebars should also be within comfortable reach.

Cross-country skiing. In terms of total body fitness, cross-country skiing is often touted as the number one form of cardiovascular exercise. Before the increased availability of treadmills and other indoor aerobic machines, many runners cross-country skied to maintain their fitness during the icy winter months when running was impractical. Today, anyone can use cross-country skiing for cross-training. Whether you ski indoors on a machine or outdoors on a real pair of skis, it provides a great cardiovascular workout and strengthens both the legs and the arms without any impact.

Many ski areas offer low-cost lessons. Proper form is crucial for obtaining exercise benefits (and enjoyment) from cross-country skiing.

Stair-climbing. Since climbing stairs and stair machines use many of the same muscles as running, neither activity should be used as cross-training to give running muscles a rest. Stair-climbing is, however, a good low-impact choice for developing a high level of aerobic conditioning and simulating hill running. When using a stair machine, always let your arms move in the natural running motion. Don't lean forward on the console or hold onto the arm rails. If you can't maintain balance or pace without holding on, adjust the speed, resistance, and/or stair height.

Swimming. As a non-weight-bearing sport, swimming offers several key advantages for cross-training. It is an especially good recovery workout because the lower extremity muscles are used differently. Swimming is also an excellent activity for strengthening the upper body, something most runners need. Unfortunately, some skill and endurance are required to use the sport for aerobic conditioning. If you have convenient access to a swimming pool, consider taking a few lessons at a local YMCA or master's swimming group.

CROSS-TRAINING PRINCIPLES TO KEEP IN MIND

Regardless of the aerobic activity you choose for cross-training, always follow the same basic training principles as your primary sport.

1. *Do a warm-up and cool-down* and increase your training gradually. Overuse injuries can occur during cross-training if the body doesn't have time to adapt to a new activity.

2. *Cross-train in moderation* but with consistency to reduce the risk of injury.

3. *Never assume* fitness in one sport automatically carries over into another. Every activity has its own set of sport-specific skills and adaptations.

4. *Learn the proper technique* for cross-training sports or activities and use the appropriate equipment and attire.

STRETCHING AND FLEXIBILITY

How you move as a runner or nonrunner is determined, in large part, by the tightness of the muscles, tendons, and ligaments that are attached to your joints. The more the muscles can stretch, the greater the flexibility and range of motion.

While there is little scientific research indicating that stretching prevents injuries or improves athletic performance, good flexibility will benefit the entire skeletal and muscular system, whether you exercise or not.

I'm So-o-o-o Stiff

Why are some people naturally more flexible than others? It has to do with anatomy, age, sex, genetics, and level of physical activity.

Fortunately, flexibility—like cardiovascular endurance and muscle strength—can improve with regular practice. At the same time, it can decrease with inactivity while certain exercises like running can limit the body's ability to move through its full range of motion.

It's Never Too Late to Start Stretching

Even if you've been lax or remiss about stretching in the past, it's never too late to start, according to author Bob Anderson, an avid trail runner and mountain biker. His popular book, *Stretching*, illustrates dozens of sport-specific stretches for different activities including running.

Stretching, he stresses, is especially important as we become older and begin to lose flexibility.

"You want your body to last at a higher level. Don't even worry about trying to improve your flexibility. Maintenance is just as good as improvement," Anderson says. "The goal is to never get any stiffer than you are today."

Although there are several common stretching techniques, the "static" or stretch-and-hold method is most popular among fitness experts and athletes. The risk of injury during static stretching is

STRETCHING DOS AND DON'TS

DO

1. Ease into a new stretching program gradually.
2. Stretch regularly to counteract the reduced flexibility that tends to occur from running.
3. Warm your muscles before stretching them.
4. Stretch slowly, smoothly, and gently.
5. Select exercises that work for your individual needs and level of flexibility.
6. Perform each stretch on both sides of the body.
7. Breathe easily during each stretch.

DON'T

1. Stretch to warm up your muscles or joints.
2. Bounce during stretches.
3. Hold your breath.
4. Stretch to the point of pain.
5. Stretch seriously fatigued or extremely knotted muscles immediately. Let them relax a little first.
6. Worry about how far you can stretch.
7. Compare your flexibility to others.

STRETCHING: FREQUENTLY ASKED QUESTIONS

By now you are probably asking yourself a few questions, such as: Should I stretch before, during, or after exercise? How long do you hold each stretch? How many times a week should I stretch?

Opinions about the timing, duration, and frequency of stretching exercises are as varied as each person's needs. Anderson advocates stretching any time you feel like it, before and after physical activity and throughout the day.

The American Council on Exercise (ACE) recommends that all aerobic activity be followed by at least a few minutes of stretching. Even five minutes of stretching after exercise, they say, is better than nothing.

According to the American College of Sports Medicine (ACSM), stretching exercises can be effectively included in the warm-up and/or cool-down periods that precede and follow the aerobic conditioning phase of an exercise session.

ACSM also recommends that an overall fitness plan incorporate flexibility exercises that stretch the major muscle/tendon groups.

ACSM guidelines for static stretching include:

Frequency A minimum of two to three days per week.
Duration Ten to thirty seconds for each static stretch.
Repetitions At least four per muscle group.

Most fitness and running books explain the different stretching techniques and include illustrations or instructions of the best stretches for various sports and parts of the body.

low compared to other techniques and it's a quick, easy, effective way to maintain or improve flexibility.

If stretching is a new element in your running routine or training program, take the time to learn and practice good technique. Improper stretching can actually do more harm than not stretching at all.

The important thing, according to Anderson, is to learn how to relax and not hold your breath. Breathe out when you begin the stretch, then breathe in and out rhythmically as you hold it, he explains. Also keep the jaw relaxed and don't let the teeth touch.

Good Stretches for Runners

If too many choices make you crazy and you'd rather run than stretch, here are five simple stretches Anderson recommends for runners. The shaded areas indicate where you will feel each stretch. Always do both sides, don't bounce, and remember to breathe.

QUADRICEP/HAMSTRING STRETCH

Stand in this bent-knee position, which contracts the quadriceps and relaxes the hamstrings. Hold for thirty seconds.

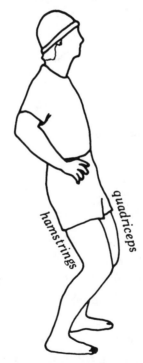

Illustratioins reprinted with permission from *Stretching* © Bob and Jean Anderson.

Because these muscles have opposing actions, tightening the quadriceps will relax the hamstrings. As you hold this bent-knee position, feel the difference between the front of the thigh (quadriceps) and the back of the thigh (hamstrings). The quadriceps should feel hard and tight while the hamstrings should feel soft and relaxed.

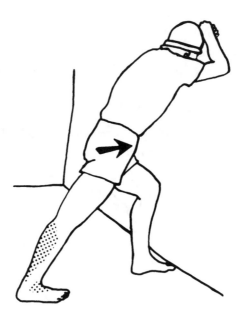

CALF STRETCH

To stretch your calf, stand a little ways from a solid support and lean on it with your forearms, head resting on your hands. Bend one leg and place your foot on the ground in front of you, leaving the other leg straight behind. Slowly move your hips forward until you feel a stretch in the calf of your straight leg. Be sure to keep the heel of the straight leg on the floor and your toes pointed straight ahead. Hold an easy stretch for thirty seconds.

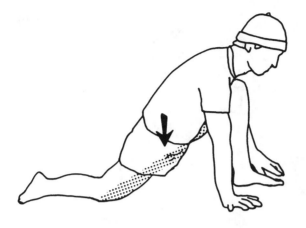

HIP/GROIN/LOWER-BACK STRETCH

Move one leg forward until the knee of the forward leg is directly over the ankle. The other knee should be resting on the floor. Without changing the position of the knee on the floor or the forward foot, lower the front hip downward to create an easy stretch. This stretch should be felt in the front of the hip and possibly in the hamstrings and groin. This will help relieve tension in the lower back. Hold the stretch for twenty to thirty seconds.

KNEE/QUAD STRETCH

Hold the top of one foot (from inside of foot) with your opposite hand and gently pull the heel toward the buttocks. The knee bends at a natural angle in this position and creates a good stretch in knee and quads.

SIDE-TO-SIDE STRETCH

With arms overhead, hold the elbow of one arm with the hand of the other arm. Keeping knees slightly bent (one inch), gently pull the elbow behind your head as you bend from the hips to the side. Hold an easy stretch for ten seconds. Keeping the knees slightly bent will provide better balance and protect your back.

STRENGTH TRAINING

For many people, a certain mystique surrounds weight or strength training and it harbors many myths and misconceptions. You don't need to look like a body builder or spend a lot of time in a weight room to benefit from strength training. Recent studies show that significant improvements in muscle strength and tone can be achieved by lifting weights for twenty to thirty minutes only two times a week.

In addition to developing a stronger musculoskeletal system, regular strength training will increase bone density and strengthen the tissues that connect to joints. These benefits help reduce the risk of injury, make daily living easier, and contribute to total body fitness. Strength training also aids in weight loss by increasing lean muscle while reducing fat and revving up your metabolism to burn more calories. As *Fit or Fat* guru Covert Bailey always explains to his audiences, fit muscles make you a "better butter burner."

Improvement Requires Overload

In order to improve muscle fitness (strength and endurance), you must progressively stress or overload the muscles beyond their normal capacity. With repeated stress, the muscles adapt and then improve their function. The type of improvement is generally determined by the amount of resistance or weight used and the number of times an exercise is repeated. In weight training, this latter number is measured in terms of repetitions and sets.

Repeating an exercise many times by doing a high number of repetitions (fifteen to twenty-five) with a light weight typically increases muscle endurance. Runners need muscle endurance because it allows the muscles to resist fatigue and keep working. Lifting a heavy weight only a few times (two to six) builds muscle strength or the ability to exert maximum force. For runners, muscle strength is important in absorbing the impact shock of landing with approximately three times your body weight. Gains in both strength and endurance, which are used for general sports training, occur with moderate weights and repetitions (eight to twelve).

Options for Building Strength

Calisthenics, free weights, and weight machines are equally good methods for building muscle strength and endurance safely, if done

Options for Building Strength

Calisthenics, free weights, and weight machines are equally good methods for building muscle strength and endurance safely, if done correctly. The most effective method is the one you'll do on a consistent basis at least two times a week.

Calisthenics. Exercises that build muscle endurance by using your own body weight for resistance are typically called calisthenics. The most common calisthenics include sit-ups, squats, push-ups, and pull-ups.

Free-weight exercises. These are performed in various positions (standing, seated, or on a bench) with handheld weights called dumbbells and barbells. A dumbbell is a short bar with weights on both ends. A barbell is a longer version of a dumbbell. Using free weights, more than one muscle group is worked at a time. The muscles can be worked from many different angles and with a variety of exercises. With proper instruction and good form, the potential for injury with free weights is relatively low.

Weight machines. We know them by their trade names: Nautilus, Cybex, and Universal. They tend to be more expensive and not as versatile as free weights. However, they are easier to use. Since machines guide your motions and movement of the weights, no special skills are required for use and the risk of injury is low. Nonetheless, it is important to obtain instructions on proper use of the equipment before beginning a program.

Who Should Weight Train?

In his book, *Run Fast: How to Train for a 5-K or 10-K Race,* Hal Higdon identifies three types of runners who probably benefit more from strength training than others. They include ectomorphs (physically slender individuals), women, and masters (men and women age forty and older).

Author Gary Moran believes all runners can benefit by using weight training to strengthen the major muscle groups and help prevent injuries.

trainer or other fitness professional who can discuss your individual needs and demonstrate proper technique and appropriate exercises for the various muscles.

In *Cross-Training for Sports,* Moran recommends that distance runners do seven (two are optional) weight-training exercises three days a week (see chart below). Different exercises emphasizing power and arm strength are recommended in the book for sprint runners.

In the beginning, Moran says, use enough weight to just complete the minimum number of repetitions. The last rep should feel somewhat challenging or difficult. As muscle fitness improves, increase the weight and/or the number of repetitions.

These five upper-body exercises and two lower-body exercises, which include a combination of calisthenics, free weights, and machines, will strengthen the muscles that benefit runners most. Runners with specific needs, as evidenced by chronic injuries, should add or substitute other strength exercises.

KEY STRENGTH EXERCISES FOR RUNNERS

Exercise	Repetitions/Set	Primary Muscles Used
Inclined dumbbell fly	1–3 sets/10 reps	Pectoralis major (chest)
Sit-ups touching alternate knees	1 set/25–75 reps	Rectus abdominis and Obliques (abdominals)
Four-way hip exercises (optional)	1 set/10 reps each exercise	Illiopsoas (hip), Adductor (groin), Gluteals (buttocks)
Leg press (optional)	1–3 sets/10 reps	Quadriceps (thigh), Gluteus maximus (buttocks)
Seated dumbbell curls	1–3 sets/10 reps	Biceps brachii, brachialis (front of upper arm)
Lateral pull-downs	1–3 sets/10 reps	Latissimus dorsi (back)
Triceps pull-downs	1–3 sets/10 reps	Triceps brachii (back of upper arm)

Guidelines for Safe and Healthy Strength-Building

To get the most out of strength workouts without risking injury, pay particular attention to proper technique and these guidelines:

- Warm up before weight training, relax between sets, and cool down after. To combine running and weights in the same workout, run first then lift.
- Exercise the large muscle groups before the smaller ones and the lower body before the upper body.
- Exhale through the nose and mouth during the effort, or lift and inhale as you return to the starting position. Never hold your breath.
- Lift and lower weights slowly and smoothly to maintain proper technique and avoid any jerking or twisting. The lift can be done to a count of "one second-two seconds" and the lower to a count of "one second–two seconds–three seconds–four seconds."

WEIGHTY WORDS

Muscle endurance   The muscle's ability to exert force repeatedly or continuously. To build endurance through weight training, use a high number of *repetitions* with light *resistance* or weight.

Muscle strength   The maximum force that a muscle can produce in a single effort. To build strength through weight training, use a low number of *repetitions* with heavy resistance or weight.

Repetition   One complete movement of an exercise. A series or group of repetitions comprises a *set*.

Resistance   The amount of force or weight used during weight training exercises.

Set   A group of *repetitions* or repeated movements of an exercise followed by a rest period.

- Allow at least one day off for recovery between weight-training sessions which use the same muscle groups.
- Keep a record of strength workouts so you don't do too much. List the specific exercises, the number of repetitions and sets, plus the amount of weight.
- Check with a doctor immediately if you experience any unusual symptoms such as dizziness, chest pains, headaches, or numbness.

RESOURCES

For more information on cross-training, strength training, and stretching/flexibility read:

Alter, Michael J. *Sport Stretch: 311 Stretches for 41 Sports.* Champaign, Ill.: Human Kinetics, 1998.

Anderson, Bob and Jean Anderson. *Stretching.* Bolinas, Calif.: Shelter Publications, 1981.

Fahey, Thomas D. *Basic Weight Training for Men & Women.* Mountain View, Calif.: Mayfield Publishing, 1997.

Moran, Gary T. and George H. McGlynn. *Cross-Training for Sports.* Champaign, Ill.: Human Kinetics, 1997.

———. *Dynamics of Strength Training and Conditioning.* Madison, Wis.: Brown & Benchmark, 1997.

Pearl, Bill and Gary T. Moran. *Getting Stronger.* Bolinas, California: Shelter Publications, 1986.

Verna, Chris and Steve Hosid. *The Complete Idiot's Guide to Healthy Stretching.* New York: Simon & Schuster, 1998.

Yacenda, John. *Fitness Cross-Training.* Champaign, Ill.: Human Kinetics, 1995.

Strength Training

For a referral to a strength-training professional in your area contact:

National Strength and Conditioning Association
PO Box 38909
Colorado Springs, CO 80937-8909
Phone: (719) 632-6722
Fax: (719) 632-6367

Stretching/Flexibility

For stretching posters, charts, bodywork tools, and other items: www.stretching.com.

For a comprehensive list of stretching references and general information on stretching and flexibility: www.enteract.com/ ~bradapp/docs/rec/stretching/

CHAPTER SEVEN

Staying Healthy as a Runner

Running, like virtually any sport, presents numerous opportunities for aches, pains, ailments, and injuries. Many of the most common maladies, such as blisters and black toenails, are a nuisance but not debilitating. A chronic injury that is ignored, however, may eventually require a complete layoff from running or perhaps surgery. More serious problems like heatstroke or hypothermia can be deadly.

Although it sounds simple, the best treatment for staying healthy as a runner is P-R-E-V-E-N-T-I-O-N. Most running ailments and injuries can be prevented entirely or easily if treated in the early stages. By being aware of potential problems or risk factors and taking a proactive approach, you can stay healthier and choose your own nonrunning days rather than letting them choose you.

MOTHER NATURE DOESN'T RUN

If every day were calm, crystal-clear, and fifty-five degrees, the world would have a lot more runners. Unfortunately, Mother Nature doesn't run and the weather she bestows upon us is not always ideal for running. Not only can the weather affect how you feel mentally during a run, it can also impact you physically.

BAD AIR DAYS

In many cities and urban settings, vehicle emissions and other forms of air pollution are an unavoidable, everyday occurrence. Federal standards identify unhealthy air days when you should refrain from outdoor exercise, but air pollution affects each person differently.

According to air-quality expert Lori Kobza-Lee, the safest time to exercise or run is early morning before air pollution is at its highest levels. In most areas throughout the country, she notes, the peak time for pollution occurs in the late afternoon and early evening. Exposure to air pollution may result in any number of symptoms including a burning sensation in the lungs, headache, watering eyes, and difficulty taking deep breaths.

"Over time, repeated exposure to unhealthy air makes you more susceptible to serious respiratory illnesses and even heart disease," says Kobza-Lee. "Athletes are particularly at risk because they suck in a lot more air than nonactive people."

In some communities residents can call a hotline for current air-quality information, and air advisories are distributed to the media during particularly hazardous periods. If your community offers one of these services, check the air quality before exercising outdoors and consider postponing a run if air pollution levels are high.

You can take an active part in improving air quality where you live by following these "Spare the Air" tips offered by the Sacramento Metropolitan Air Quality Management District:

- Reduce, postpone, or eliminate all unnecessary driving.
- Consolidate trips.
- Limit use of aerosols.
- Ride a bike/walk/run.
- Purchase a reduced-emission vehicle.
- Avoid using charcoal lighter fluid.
- Get regular auto tune-ups.
- Take the bus/light rail.
- Car- or vanpool.
- Keep your vehicle's tires properly inflated.

Precautions for Hot-Weather Running

Running in extreme weather conditions—either hot or cold—can be dangerous if you are not aware of the potential hazards and precautions to avoid them.

Here are a few special hot-weather running tips provided by the Road Runners Club of America (RRCA).

1. *Avoid dehydration!* You can lose between six and twelve ounces of fluids for every twenty minutes of running. Therefore, it is important to prehydrate (ten to fifteen ounces of fluid ten to fifteen minutes prior to running) and drink fluids every twenty to thirty minutes along your running route. To determine if you are hydrating properly, weigh yourself before and after running. You should have drunk one pint of fluid for every pound you're missing. Indicators that you are running dehydrated are a persistent elevated pulse rate after finishing your run, and dark-yellow urine. Keep in mind that thirst is not an adequate indicator of dehydration.

2. *Run in the shade whenever possible;* avoid direct sun and blacktops. When you are going to be exposed to sunlight apply at least an SPF 15 sunscreen. Not only can the sun affect your skin but its rays can affect your eyes, so when it is sunny wear sunglasses that can filter out UVA and UVB rays. Wearing a hat with a visor will not only shade your eyes but can also protect the skin on your face.

3. *When running, if you become* dizzy, nauseated, have dry skin, or the chills . . . stop running and get a drink. If you do not feel better, get help.

4. *If you have a heart or respiratory problem* or are on any medication, consult with your doctor about running in the heat. In some cases it may be in your best interest to run indoors. Also, if you have a history of heatstroke or related illnesses, run with extreme caution.

5. *Children should limit their running* in the heat due to their lower tolerance.

6. *Avoid plastic sweat suits,* late-morning races, salt tablets, and drinks with high sugar concentration. Avoid running ill.

7. *Wear light-colored clothing,* check hair and body for ticks after running in the woods, drink plenty of water, listen to the race

director's prerace announcements regarding the heat/ humidity, and tell someone your running route.

Tips for Cold-Weather Running

There's no need to let winter curb outdoor running, if you prepare properly for the inclement weather. The following cold-weather running precautions are also offered by RRCA:

1. *Wear clothing in layers* so that warm air can be trapped between the layers. Depending on the weather conditions, two to four layers on the trunk and one to two layers on the legs are appropriate. It is helpful if the outer layers have vents and zippers to allow excess heat to escape as you become warm. On windy days the outer layer should be of wind-resistant material.

2. *Clothing made of material* which carries the sweat away from the body is best, like wool, silk, or "space-age" synthetics like polypropylene or polyester. Avoid cotton as it tends to hold the sweat.

3. *Hat and gloves are crucial* as these regions of the body have a substantial role in the regulation of body temperature. Mittens tend to be warmer than gloves. On very cold days mittens worn over gloves are effective. Stocking caps or ski masks are desirable. On windy days goggles or eyeglasses can provide additional protection.

4. *The outer layer should be light-colored* and include reflective material if you are running during darker hours. Reflective material works only if there is a light source; for example, blaze orange becomes poorly visible brown at night. Light-colored material is visible even without a strong light source. During snowy days dark colors provide visible contrast and attract solar energy.

5. *Pin to your clothes or shoes emergency identification,* preferably of a waterproof material. Let someone know where you are going to run and when you expect to return. Do not run with headphones.

6. *Plan to run into the wind* during the beginning portions and with the wind behind you in the latter portions. Otherwise built-up sweat may make you too cold when you turn into the wind. Be alert when running in snowy, icy conditions particularly near vehicular traffic.

7. *Avoid overdressing.* Feel a bit underdressed and chilly as you start, knowing that later as you run in your layered environment the temperature will rise about twenty degrees.

INJURIES ARE NOT INEVITABLE

According to New York podiatrist Douglas F. Tumen, an American Running and Fitness Association (ARFA) advisor, the arch and heel region, lower leg, knee, Achilles tendon, and forefoot are the most commonly injured areas. Overuse, faulty biomechanics, and lack of flexibility, he also notes, usually cause running injuries.

(A running injury is rarely a total surprise to the injured runner. In all likelihood, the injury was preceded by weeks or even months of a low-level nagging problem like a tight muscle or soreness.) Since minor symptoms aren't particularly painful or debilitating in the beginning, many runners put them out of their minds and continue running. Eventually, when the body can't protect the area anymore and the stress is too high, it breaks down.

In the *Healthy Runner's Handbook,* authors Lyle J. Micheli and Mark Jenkins note that the risk factors associated with overuse injuries can be attributed to both intrinsic and extrinsic elements. The intrinsic ones relate to the individual runner and include such risk factors as anatomical abnormalities, poor conditioning, and incorrect running technique. The extrinsic risk factors are associated with the sport itself and include training errors, improper footwear, and inappropriate workout structure.

(By recognizing and addressing the risk factors, you can significantly reduce the chance of an overuse injury. Sometimes injury prevention is as simple as adding specific stretches or strength-training exercises, changing shoes, or doing a better warm-up. Is it possible to run without becoming injured? Micheli and Jenkins say yes, "so long as the runner takes precautions and becomes familiar with self-management techniques."

To reduce your risk of overuse injury, ARFA offers these guidelines:

- Build mileage slowly. Increase by no more than 10 percent a week or 20 percent every two weeks.
- Follow hard days with easy recovery days.
- Do not routinely increase your weekly mileage. Plan easy and hard weeks.
- Cross-train. Replacing a day of running with swimming, bicycling, in-line skating, or stair-climbing will give you an aerobic workout while resting running muscles.
- The risk of overuse injuries rises dramatically as your weekly mileage goes above forty to fifty miles. Maintain this level only if you can do so relatively pain-free.
- Racing places enormous stress on the body. Plan a racing schedule that allows enough recovery between events. Run easy at least one day for each mile of a race.

Signs of Injury

The three most common signs of injury are inflammation (swelling and bruising); loss of function; and pain that continues through a run or several days in a row.

The last thing most runners want to do under any circumstances is stop running. When plagued with an injury, that's often exactly what you need to do. Discussing injuries in *Better Runs*, author Joe Henderson notes, "The loss of running hurts worse than the injury." Refusing to accept that loss, failing to wait out the pain, rushing the recovery timetable, and neglecting to correct the causes, he says, all prolong and intensify the pain. His point is well-taken.

Fortunately, most running injuries are relatively minor. Comparing them to high-cost, major-trauma football injuries, Henderson says the problems most runners talk about rank in severity with headaches and toothaches.

Most common running injuries, according to runner and physical therapist Lisa Glaser, rarely require more than RICE, a self-treatment consisting of Rest, Ice, Compression, and Elevation. Nonsteroid, anti-inflammatory drugs like aspirin and ibuprofen, called NSAIDs, she adds, can also be helpful if recommended by a physician.

You should, however, seek immediate medical intervention for sharp, stabbing, unrelenting pain in any joint. Never try to run through pain that forces you to limp or adapt your gait. It may only make the problem worse or create new ones. A medical evaluation, Glaser says, may also be necessary for dull aches and joint discomfort that persist more than a week after self-treatment and modifications in exercise are made.

Many medical and health professionals offer services for prevention, treatment, and rehabilitation of running injuries. Although managed care may limit your choice of providers, try to seek referrals to sports-medicine specialists who are runners or know running. They're more familiar with the idiosyncrasies of the sport and tend to understand the need to continue or quickly resume running.

Depending on the type of injury, treatment and rehabilitation may include nonrunning activities. Rest, the "R" in the RICE formula, doesn't necessarily mean inactivity and no exercise at all. Ask your doctor or health practitioner what you can do for exercise and then stay as active as possible.

MASSAGE

Fortunately for runners and other athletes, the massage parlors of the past have given way to a new era of professionals who are trained to provide therapeutic massage to help a wide range of

> **HOT OR COLD?**
>
> For many injured runners, the thought of soaking in a warm bath or wrapping a heating pad around an injury is a lot more appealing than applying ice or jumping into a cold bath. If you're confused about whether ice or heat is the best treatment for an injury, pick ice and you'll rarely go wrong. Ice will deaden the pain and reduce swelling by preventing the blood from circulating deep in the tissues where bleeding may occur. Heat is a valuable aid in restoring blood flow to an injured area but wait a few days until swelling subsides. After the third day or so, alternating treatments of ice and heat are often recommended, provided the session ends with ice.

medical conditions including pulled or strained muscles, sprained ligaments, and other sports injuries.

There are many forms of massage including sports massage, which focuses on muscle groups relevant to the particular sport. In their brochure, "Enhancing Your Health with Therapeutic Massage," the American Massage Therapy Association classifies sports massage therapy into three main categories:

1. *Maintenance massage* is a regular program designed to help the athlete reach optimal performance through injury-free training.

2. *Event massage* enhances the body's recovery process, improving the athlete's return to high-level training and competition, and reducing the risk of injury.

3. *Rehabilitation massage* manages both acute and chronic injuries.

Even if you can't have a professional massage on a regular basis, a trained massage therapist can teach you self-massage techniques.

WHEN TRAINING IS OVERDONE

Like overuse injuries, overtraining doesn't happen as the result of any one specific workout. It occurs after weeks or months of run-

---

TOENAIL TALK

Many runners assume that black toenails (and losing your toenails altogether) are the inevitable result of high mileage and lots of downhill running. That's not true, although both factors can contribute to foot-related problems.

Always make sure your shoes fit properly. As mentioned in chapter two, it is generally recommended that you have at least one thumb's width of space from the end of your longest toe to the end of the shoe when standing. The extra room will accommodate a foot that swells from hours of pounding.

The extra space, however, won't always prevent black toenails. "You can have six inches of extra space and still get black toenails," says California podiatrist David Hannaford, a sports-medicine and running-injury specialist. "The real reason toenails get black is microtrauma." The best prevention, he says, is to trim and file the toenails at least once a week.

According to Hannaford, a long-distance runner, toenails should be trimmed short so they do not extend beyond the end of the toes. The front of each nail should then be filed smooth using a downward motion to bevel the edge. Smooth all the rough spots but don't file or trim the corners inward.

---

ning too many miles or too many hard workouts and not taking off enough time. Unlike many running injuries, which display distinctive symptoms, overtraining is characterized by a long list of symptoms, many of which are rather nebulous.

Some of the physical signs of overtraining include:

- Fatigue and prolonged recovery
- Decreased performance
- Elevated morning heart rate
- Staleness
- Loss of appetite
- Muscle and joint soreness/tenderness

- Loss of coordination
- Irritability
- Decreased ability to fight infection
- Sleep disturbances

In their *Fit Facts* flier, *Too Much of a Good Thing,* the American Council on Exercise notes that not all signs of overtraining are physical. Psychological and emotional signs of overtraining include:

- Apathy
- Depression
- Concentration difficulties
- Reduced self-esteem
- Emotional sensitivity

By identifying the signs of overtraining early, you can adapt your training and reduce the risk of a chronic problem. Start by getting more sleep and cutting your training time in half for a few days or substituting some runs with cross-training. If you don't see a change, eliminate training days altogether. Go back to your training log and identify when you began doing too much. When you feel well enough to increase your running, do so gradually.

RESOURCES

Injuries and Sports Medicine

For more information on injury treatment and prevention read:

Ellis, Joe. *Running Injury-Free: How to Prevent, Treat and Recover from Dozens of Painful Problems.* Emmaus, Pa: Rodale Press, 1994.

Julien, Perry H. *Sure Footing: A Sports Podiatrist's Perspective on Running and Exercise-Related Injuries.* Atlanta, Ga.: Atlanta Food and Ankle Center, 1998.

Micheli, Lyle J. with Mark Jenkins. *Healthy Runner's Handbook.* Champaign, Ill.: Human Kinetics, 1996.

Moffat, Marilyn and Steve Vickery. *The American Physical Therapy Association Book of Body Maintenance and Repair.* New York: Henry Holt and Company, 1999.

Shangold, Mona M. and Gabe Mirkin. *The Complete Sports Medicine Book for Women.* New York: Simon & Schuster, 1992.

Vonhof, John. *Fixing Your Feet.* Mukilteo, Wash.: WinePress Publishing, 1997.

For subscription information on *The Penn State Sports Medicine Newsletter,* a monthly publication on sports injuries, conditioning, safety, and nutrition, contact:

The Penn State Sports Newsletter
PO Box 3073
Dept. SM
Langhorne, PA 19047-9377
Phone: (215) 788-8424

For consumer and professional information on various sports-medicine topics including training and treatment:

American College of Sports Medicine (ACSM)
PO Box 1440
Indianapolis, IN 46206
Phone: (317) 637-9200
Web site: www.acsm.org/sportsmed

ACSM is a professional association of medical and allied health professionals who support the research of and advancement in sports medicine and exercise science.

To obtain free literature on more than thirty foot health-care topics, call the American Podiatric Medical Association (APMA) toll-free information center:

1-800-FOOTCARE

APMA is a national association of podiatrists with individual societies in all fifty states, the District of Columbia, and Puerto Rico. (AAPSM is an affiliate of APMA.)

American Podiatric Medical Association (APMA)
9312 Old Georgetown Rd.
Bethesda, MD 20114
Phone: (301) 571-9200

American Academy of Podiatric Sports Medicine (AAPSM)
1729 Glastonberry Rd.
Potomac, MD 20864
Phone: 1-800-438-3355 or (301) 424-7440
Web site: www.aapsm.org

For referrals to orthopaedic surgeons:

American Academy of Orthopaedic Surgeons
6300 N. River Rd.
Rosemont, IL 60018
Phone: 1-800-346-AAOS
Fax: (847) 823-8125
Web site: www.aaos.org

For referrals to licensed practicing physicians whose primary interest is sports medicine:

American Academy of Sports Physicians
17113 Gledhill St.
Northridge, CA 91325
Phone: (818) 886-7891

For referrals to orthopaedists (medical doctors) specializing in foot care:

American Orthopaedic Foot and Ankle Society
1216 Pine St., Suite 201
Seattle, WA 98101
Phone: 1-800-235-4855 or (206) 223-1120
Fax: (206) 223-1178
E-mail: aofas@aofas.org
Web site: www.aofas.org

For information about physical therapy and physical therapists in your area contact:

American Physical Therapy Association (APTA)
1111 N. Fairfax St.
Alexandria, VA 22314-1488
Phone: (703) 684-APTA
Web site: www.apta.org

APTA is a national professional organization representing more than 75,000 physical therapists, physical-therapist assistants, and students in the United States.

For free copies of the following APTA brochures send a self-addressed, stamped envelope to the above address.

Taking Care of Your Knees
Taking Care of Your Foot and Ankle
Fitness: A Way of Life
Why it Feels Right to Put Your Health in the Hands of a Physical Therapist.

For on-line information on prevention and treatment of running injuries:

Dr. Stephen M. Pribut's Sports Pages:
www.clark.net/pub/pribut/spinjur
FootWeb: www.footweb.com
The Physician and Sportsmedicine: www.physsportsmed.com
Runner's World Online: www.runnersworld.com/injuries
Sports Medicine and Orthopedic Surgery—Dr. Stuart Zeman:
www.sports-medicine.com
SportsMedWeb: www.rice.edu/~jenky

Massage, Yoga

For information on sports massage and yoga read:

Couch, Jean. *The Runner's Yoga Book.* Berkeley, Calif.: Rodmell Press, 1990.

Johnson, Joan. *The Healing Art of Sports Massage.* Emmaus, Pa.: Rodale Press, 1995.

King, Robert K. *Performance Massage.* Champaign, Ill.: Human Kinetics, 1993.

Pike, Gregory. *Sports Massage for Peak Performance.* New York: HarperPerennial, 1997.

To receive a free copy of the pamphlet *Enhancing Your Health with Therapeutic Massage* or to locate a qualified massage therapist in your area, contact:

American Massage Therapy Association
820 Davis St., Suite 100
Evanston, IL 60201-4444
Phone: (847) 864-0123
Fax: (847) 864-1178
E-mail: info@inet.amtamassage.org
Web site: www.amtamassage.org

Air Quality

To find the agency charged with air-quality responsibilities in your community, call STAPPA/ALAPCO (State and Territorial Air Pollution Program Administrators/Association of Local Air Pollution Control Officials) at (202) 624-7864.

CHAPTER EIGHT

Fueling Up To Run

Most runners really like to eat. Many who picked at their food before becoming runners soon discover they actually had to eat more to maintain the energy to run. Overweight folks who turned to running to slim down are elated to find out they can maintain reasonable weights and still eat without dieting. Hence the saying, "Runners eat to run and run to eat."

How the body breaks down and uses food for energy or fuel and other purposes is a matter of chemistry. If you skipped chemistry in school, here's a nonscientific explanation.

The energy we need to perform necessary body functions, run, and do other activities comes from food that contains carbohydrates, fats, and proteins (and alcohol for those who drink). The energy, measured in terms of calories, is held in the chemical bonds of these compounds. As the need for energy arises it is released and used by cells in the body. The compounds in food also provide all the vital, life-sustaining nutrients we need for good health.

You don't need to understand any more of that process except that the *basic* nutritional requirements are about the same for every body—athlete or otherwise. The energy (caloric) needs, however, will vary because most active people who run around for work and play need more energy than those who spend their time sitting at a desk and in front of the television.

SEEK SOUND NUTRITIONAL ADVICE

Nothing in this chapter is intended to be a substitute for sound nutritional advice available from your doctor or a registered dietitian. Many health-and-fitness professionals, such as the Lifestyle and Weight Management Consultants certified by the American Council on Exercise, can teach general principles of healthy eating and exercise but they are not qualified to "prescribe" diets or provide nutritional services under the legal purview of other medical or health-care professionals.

As of early 1999, according to the American Dietetic Association (ADA), thirty-eight states had laws regulating dietitians and nutritionists. When seeking nutritional services, review the individual's credentials to ensure proper registration, certification, or licensing in your state, as well as their qualifications to provide the services you need.

The Essentials

A healthy diet requires six essentials—carbohydrates, fat, protein, vitamins, minerals, and water. Collectively they help build and maintain the body, regulate metabolic functions, and provide energy.

Carbohydrates. Sometimes called "carbos," are found primarily in fruits, vegetables, grains, and pasta. They are the body's most efficient and readily available source of energy. Carbos are also the only fuel we eat that can support anaerobic activities such as running hard. In addition to helping fuel the muscles during aerobic activity, carbohydrates fuel the brain and the nervous system.

It is generally recommended that runners and other athletes obtain at least 60 percent of their total calories from carbohydrates. Since the body only stores a small amount of carbohydrates (unlike fat), you must keep the supplies replenished.

Protein. The body's major building material. Muscles, the brain, skin, hair, and connective tissues are composed primarily of protein. Even important components of the blood, cell membranes, and the immune systems come from proteins. Very little protein is used to fuel muscles but it can contribute to energy needs during endurance exercise and other aerobic activity. According to the pamphlet, *Nutrition for Performance: An Athlete's*

Guide to Smart Eating by the American Running and Fitness Association, athletes should get 12 to 15 percent of their total daily calories from protein.

Although many people think of meat, fish, and poultry as the only sources of protein, it is found in many different types of food such as grains and legumes.

Fat. Of the six nutrients, fat has gotten a bad rap. Fat is absolutely essential to a healthy diet but only a small amount is required, the equivalent of less than one tablespoon per day. You do not need to eat extra fat because it is found in many foods. One key function of fat is carrying the fat-soluble vitamins (A, D, E, and K) into the body for various uses. At rest, the muscles burn primarily fat for energy needs. Stored body fat can also be a source of energy during endurance events.

Most of us recognize the obvious forms of fat (lard, margarine, butter, and oil) but other foods are also high in fat. In general, foods that come from animals are naturally higher in fat than those that come from plants. Avocados, olives, nuts, and seeds, all high in fat, are exceptions to that rule.

Vitamins and minerals. These do not provide energy or contain calories but they are essential to the body. The main role of vitamins—a minimum of thirteen are needed by humans—is to regulate and support chemical reactions in the body. Although the body can synthesize or make small amounts of some vitamins, most required vitamins come from plant and animal sources.

Minerals are critical to the body's nervous system, metabolic processes, water balance, and the structural systems. Although plant foods are the best sources of minerals like copper, the best dietary mineral sources are animal products, especially seafood.

By eating a variety of foods and a reasonable amount for your body's energy needs, you will probably meet your body's requirements for vitamins and minerals. There are individual variations; Deficiencies in certain vitamins and minerals can be harmful, as can excessive intake or buildup of others.

IRON DEFICIENCY IS COMMON

According to the *Journal of the American Medical Association,* research indicates that 7.8 million women of child-bearing age and adolescent girls have an iron deficiency or low levels of iron stores. Some of these cases, if not recognized and treated, can lead to iron-deficiency anemia.

Iron, a mineral, is of special importance to athletes because it helps red blood cells carry oxygen to the muscles. If less oxygen is delivered to the cells, you'll lack energy and feel tired or weak. Iron also forms new red blood cells and helps the body fight infection by producing antibodies.

Athletes, particularly women, should pay attention to their iron intake because:

- Iron is lost in menstruation and sweat.
- Iron requirements increase for the enhanced red-blood-cell production associated with athletic fitness.
- Foot strike destroys red blood cells (red cells are broken by the trauma created as they pass through the blood vessels in the foot when it strikes the ground during exercise).

When lost iron is not replenished it can eventually lead to iron-deficiency anemia and impaired endurance.

Including iron-rich foods in your diet is the easiest way to keep iron levels adequate. The type of iron found in animals (lean red meat, dark poultry, and clams are all high in iron) can be used by the body more readily than iron found in plant sources such as legumes. Check with your doctor before taking iron supplements because an overabundance of iron can be toxic.

Water is Key

Last but not least, your body requires **water**. Water is considered the single most important nutrient because it is absolutely essential. The body can go weeks without food, but it can only survive about seven days without water.

Making up more than 50 percent of our bodies, water is involved in almost all body functions. Among other duties, water transports nutrients and waste, lubricates joints, and regulates body temperature. The average person needs at least eight cups of water (sixty-four ounces) a day and someone who runs and exercises should add another one to three cups for each hour of activity.

If you don't stay adequately hydrated during exercise, training, and racing, your heart rate will increase and your ability to perform physically and mentally will decrease rapidly.

WHAT IS A HEALTHY DIET FOR RUNNERS?

Runners and athletes can get a healthy diet by following the same principles recommended for all Americans. According to the U.S. Department of Agriculture's Food Guide Pyramid, which illustrates the ideal standard for a healthy, balanced diet, you should:

- Eat a variety of foods.
- Choose a diet with plenty of vegetables, fruits, and grains.
- Keep your diet low in fat, saturated fat, and cholesterol.
- Consume sugars in moderation.

Three additional dietary guidelines are also recommended by the USDA but not represented in the Food Guide Pyramid:

1. *Use salt* in moderation.
2. *Drink alcohol* in moderation, if you drink at all.
3. *Maintain* a healthy weight.

Food Guide Pyramid

A Guide to Daily Food Choices

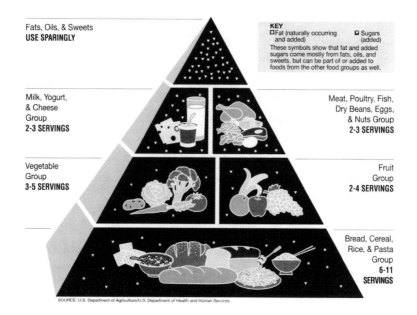

Fats, Oils, & Sweets
USE SPARINGLY

KEY
□ Fat (naturally occurring and added)   ◪ Sugars (added)
These symbols show that fat and added sugars come mostly from fats, oils, and sweets, but can be part of or added to foods from the other food groups as well.

Milk, Yogurt, & Cheese Group
2-3 SERVINGS

Meat, Poultry, Fish, Dry Beans, Eggs, & Nuts Group
2-3 SERVINGS

Vegetable Group
3-5 SERVINGS

Fruit Group
2-4 SERVINGS

Bread, Cereal, Rice, & Pasta Group
6-11 SERVINGS

SOURCE: U.S. Department of Agriculture/U.S. Department of Health and Human Services

How Many Servings Do Runners Need?

Everyone should eat at least the minimum number of servings shown in the pyramid (1,600 calories per day). Your level of exercise and activity will determine whether you need more than the minimum. Anyone who exercises vigorously on a regular basis, like most runners, should be at the upper end of the range (2,800 calories per day). High-mileage runners may need even more. Runners must eat an adequate number of calories to support their bodies' demands for energy or their performances will suffer.

The key to using the Food Guide Pyramid effectively is knowing what constitutes one serving. It is smaller than many people realize. For example, six to eleven servings of bread, cereal, rice, and pasta may seem like a lot until you know that one serving is equal to:

½ of a bagel or English muffin
1 ounce of dry cereal
½ cup of cooked rice or pasta
5–6 small crackers

Don't Run on Empty

By following the basic principles of healthy eating, you'll get all the necessary nutrients and calories your body needs for everyday living and exercising. Eating to compete, however, is a different story. High-intensity and high-endurance activities like road racing put special demands on the body and its fuel-burning system.

Detailed explanations about what to eat before, during, and after an event can be found in any sports-nutrition book (see resources) and a few basic guidelines are included here. Nutritional theories are always changing as the most current knowledge is applied to the practical aspects of training and racing. Experiment with different foods and timing to determine what works for your body and the duration and intensity of your running.

According to *Nancy Clark's Sports Nutrition Guidebook,* a 150-pound active male has about 1,800 calories of stored carbohydrates and more than 60,000 calories of stored fat. But carbohydrates, Clark says, are the limiting factor for endurance athletes because the muscles need a minimum amount to function well.

During and After a Race

Manufacturers of sports drinks, bars, gels, and other nutritional items would like us to believe their products are essential to top performance. Unfortunately, a lot of the related research is self-sponsored and biased. We do know that exercising muscles need carbohydrate energy and the body must stay properly hydrated. You can do that with food and water, sports drinks and sports products, or any combination of these items that work.

EATING DOS AND DON'TS BEFORE A RACE

DO eat two to four hours before your event. Preevent meals should help prevent hunger and keep blood-sugar levels normal.

DO select high-carbohydrate, low-fat foods. Quality high-carbohydrate foods will fuel muscles while high-fat foods, which are hard to digest, may contribute to sluggishness.

DO avoid high-fiber and gas-producing foods. Gastrointestinal distress is the last thing you need during a race.

DO keep portions moderate. The more you eat before a race, the longer it will take to digest.

DO drink at least sixteen ounces of fluid approximately two hours before a race and another sixteen ounces twenty minutes before.

DON'T overeat the night before the event.

DON'T try any food or drink you haven't tested during training.

DON'T drink alcohol, tea, or coffee. While these beverages supply water they also are diuretics which increase water output and increase water needs.

For races that last less than an hour, plain old water is usually adequate if you drink enough—five to ten fluid ounces every fifteen to twenty minutes. Don't rely on thirst as an indicator of fluid needs. You can lose as much as two quarts of fluid before the brain signals thirst. Always drink as much water as possible at every aid station, especially the early ones.

After about sixty minutes, a sport drink or food can aid performance by sustaining the body's glucose levels and replacing lost fluids faster than water. Although many drinks contain sodium and electrolytes, these components aren't necessary unless the event

THE SKINNY ON FAT

Fat. It's a burning issue. Everyone wants to lose it, burn it, and eat less of it. Although the body needs some fat to function efficiently, most of us eat too much. According to current estimates, the typical diet in the United States is 35 to 40 percent fat. It is also estimated that one-third of U.S. residents are overweight.

Fat is Essential

How much fat we need is a matter of considerable controversy. The American Heart Association suggests that less than 30 percent of total calories should come from fat. In his popular book, *Eat More Weigh Less,* Dean Ornish advocates whittling daily fat intake down to a skinny 10 percent. Sports nutritionist Nancy Clark recommends that sports-active people aim for a diet that's 25 percent fat.

Fat-Burning

One major area of confusion about fat-burning is whether low-intensity exercises like walking burn more fat than high-intensity exercises like running.

The body will take and use whatever type of calorie it can based on each individual's fitness level and the intensity of the activity. At low intensities the body burns a high percentage of fat for fuel but the total calories burned per hour is relatively small. At higher intensities, the percentage of fat being burned is lower but the total number of calories burned is much higher.

If this is confusing, think of fat-burning as a pie. At low intensity, the pie is almost all fat but the pie itself is one of those small, single-serving portions. At higher intensities, the pie may be only half fat but the pie serves six. Do you want to burn an entire single-serving pie or half of a six-serving pie?

(Continued)

Fit individuals have higher metabolic rates than unfit people so they expend more energy and burn more calories even at rest. Their bodies are also able to use more stored fat for energy as the fit body "spares" the use of carbohydrates.

Unfortunately, overweight people are more fat-efficient and they burn fat calories more sparingly than those who are normal weight. Since unfit or deconditioned people can't exercise very long at a high intensity, they should start out exercising mostly at lower intensities and longer duration to burn a higher number of total calories. They will then be more likely to continue exercising and as fitness improves, the intensity and duration can increase.

Instead of worrying about which fuel you burn during exercise, most nutritionists and fitness professionals recommend paying attention to the amount of exercise and the quantity and quality of the food you eat. Any excess calories (fat, protein, or carbohydrate) that aren't used will be stored as body fat—approximately one pound of fat for every 3,500 excess calories! Just ten extra calories a day (one stick of gum or piece of hard candy) adds up to nearly a pound in one year.

The Fallacy of Fat-Free

Many people make the mistake of thinking fat-free foods are the key to losing weight. Fat-free does not necessarily mean calorie-free. Most fat-free replacement foods have just as many calories as their regular fat-laden versions. And sodium and other chemical substances are often added to fat-free foods to give them more flavor and texture.

lasts more than a couple of hours. It is generally suggested that a sports beverage contain no more than fifty to eighty calories per eight ounces or it may not be absorbed properly. Sports bars, gels, and food items like bananas don't replace fluids but they do provide energy and keep hunger pangs at bay during long races. Drink plenty of water with bars and gels to help the body absorb them.

Every body tolerates food and drink differently. The key is to find products that taste good and work for you without upsetting your gastrointestinal system. Be sure to test all foods and drink during training runs.

After an endurance event, you can speed the recovery by eating and drinking a little something as soon as possible. Research indicates that there is a fifteen- to thirty-minute "carbohydrate window of opportunity" when the muscles are more receptive to being refueled. Try to get several hundred calories of carbohydrates into your system immediately after a long endurance race or run and drink at least sixteen ounces of fluid for each pound of weight lost during the activity.

RESOURCES

For information on eating to fuel an active lifestyle read:

Applegate, Liz. *Power Foods*. Emmaus, Pa.: Rodale Press, 1991.
Clark, Nancy. *Nancy Clark's Sports Nutrition Guidebook*. Champaign, Ill.: Human Kinetics, 1997.
Coleman, Ellen. *Eating for Endurance*. Palo Alto, Calif.: Bull Publishing, 1997.
Kleiner, Susan with Maggie Greenwood Robinson. *Power Eating*. Champaign, Ill.: Human Kinetics, 1998.

A copy of the **Good Nutrition Reading List,** the American Dietetic Association's summary of the top one hundred nutrition books and newsletters, is available on-line: www.eatright.org. A printed list may be purchased by sending a self-addressed, stamped, business-size envelope and $3.50 check to:

ADAF—Good Nutrition Reading List
PO Box 77-6034
Chicago, IL 60678-6034

For reliable nutrition information on the Internet, check: www.navigator.tufts.edu. Created by Jeanne Goldberg, a nutrition professor at Tufts University, the site helps consumers sort through information by rating two hundred Web pages covering nutrition topics.

For practical, timely, food and nutrition messages in English or Spanish, call: 1-800-366-1655, Monday through Friday from 8 A.M. to 8 P.M. CST.

For a referral to a qualified dietitian in your area:

American Dietetic Association
216 W. Jackson Blvd.
Chicago, IL 60606
Phone: 1-800-366-1655

To ask a registered dietitian a personal food or nutrition question call: 1-800-225-5267 or CALL-AN-RD, Monday through Friday from 9 A.M. to 4 P.M. CST. There is a per-minute fee for this service.

For a free copy of the pamphlet, *Iron! The Oxygen Mover Energy Booster,* send a self-addressed, stamped envelope to:

California Beef Council
5726 Sonoma Dr., Suite A
Pleasanton, CA 94566

For a free copy of the pamphlet, *Nutrition for Performance: An Athlete's Guide to Eating Smart,* send a self-addressed, stamped (55¢) envelope to:

American Running and Fitness Association
4405 East West Hwy., Suite 405
Bethesda, MD 20814

For a free copy of *Stay Cool to Perform Your Best,* a brochure that addresses the importance of including fluids in your daily exercise routine, send a self-addressed, stamped envelope to:

American College of Sports Medicine
c/o Public Information
PO Box 1440
Indianapolis, IN 46206-1440

To order a copy of the USDA's *The Food Guide Pyramid* book-let, send a one dollar check or money order made out to the Superintendent of Documents to:

Consumer Information Center
Department 159-Y
Pueblo, CO 81009

CHAPTER NINE

Running the Heart Way

Imagine a watchlike device which helps you run faster, lose fat, and improve health and fitness—all for less than a hundred dollars. Sound too good to be true? The device is called a heart rate monitor.

Just a decade ago, heart rate monitors were used by only a handful of top-level athletes. Aspiring to the highest levels of performance and willing to embrace a technology formerly limited to medical and laboratory settings, these athletes became early pioneers in a revolutionary training concept based on effort as indicated by heart rate, not time.

One of these pioneers, multisport endurance athlete Sally Edwards, stresses that whether you run for competition, recreation, or fitness and health, a monitor will add a whole new dimension to workouts.

"A heart monitor can ensure that you'll get maximum efficiency from each and every run or workout," says Edwards, an exercise physiologist who has written three books on training with a heart rate monitor. "You can run smarter and get more return from the time and effort you spend in the gym, on the road, or at the track."

HOW DO MONITORS WORK?

Today, the most popular heart monitors for runners are wireless units which measure, display, and record the number of times your heart contracts or beats per minute (bpm). Technically, the monitor measures the time between each electrical impulse and then converts it to a heart rate number, which is an average of several readings. Obtaining a near-instantaneous reading of your heart rate this way is much faster, easier, and decidedly more accurate than the two-fingered manual method of measuring pulse.

A variety of monitoring devices are on the market. Don't confuse a heart rate monitor with a "pulse meter" which detects the heart rate signal by passing light waves through the blood vessels (usually in an earlobe or fingertip). Pulse meters are very sensitive to changes in light and are not as reliable or accurate as true heart rate monitors.

MONITOR COMPONENTS AND FEATURES

Ranging in price from less than one hundred dollars to nearly four hundred dollars, wireless units consist of three components:

1. A *chest transmitter* with electrodes that transmits heart rate signals to a receiver. Depending on the manufacturer, the transmitter may be a one-piece unit with electrodes inside or it may snap to the front of a chest strap, which contains built-in electrodes.

2. A *strap* worn around the chest to hold a transmitter in place.

3. A *wrist receiver,* which receives the heart's signal, and displays it visually as a number.

The significant variation in cost is primarily attributed to what the monitor can do—its capabilities and functions—and who manufactures it. There are literally dozens of monitors on the market offering numerous options forcing consumers to make some important decisions. If you're in the market for a monitor, shopping considerations are provided later in this chapter and a list of major manufacturers is included in the appendix.

THE BASICS OF HEART RATE MONITOR TRAINING

Training with a heart rate monitor, also known as heart zone training, is generally characterized by individualized workouts conducted at a specific heart rate (such as 145 bpm) or within a range of heart rates (140 to 150 bpm) called a zone. Each zone requires a different level of effort or exercise intensity and is measured as a percentage of an individual's maximum heart rate (Max HR).

In *Precision Running With Your Polar Electronic Heart Rate Monitor,* Roy Benson refers to three zones: Weight Management (60 to 70 percent of Max HR), Aerobic (70 to 80 percent of Max HR), and Peak Performance (80 to 100 percent of Max HR).

Edwards uses five zones in her books: Healthy Heart (50 to 60 percent of Max HR), Temperate or Weight Management (60 to 70 percent of Max HR), Aerobic (70 to 80 percent of Max HR), Anaerobic Threshold (80 to 90 percent of Max HR), and Redline (90 to 100 percent of Max HR).

Other sports-and-fitness professionals have developed different systems. The name and number of zones don't matter as much as understanding how your body responds when running or exercising at different intensity levels. Some of the physiological effects are summarized in the chart.

Knowing Your Max HR is Critical

According to *Runner's World* columnist Owen Anderson, who also publishes the monthly newsletter *Running Research News,* effective monitor training begins with determining an accurate Max HR. "Many users don't actually take the time to find out their max," he says. "The formulas, such as 220-minus your age, are not very accurate."

Maximum heart rate is the highest number of times your heart can contract in one minute; when your heart is beating as fast as it can, that is its Max HR. This one single number is the most critical piece of information needed to train and race with a heart rate monitor.

Despite decades of confusion and misinformation, it is now generally agreed that Max HR:

Heart Rate	Purpose	Body's Response
50–60% of Max HR	Beginning exercise level for individuals who are out-of-shape, new to training or have been inactive.	Provides the first health benefits like lower blood pressure and improved cholesterol levels.
60–70% of Max HR	Good for easy recovery days, long slow distance, and warm-ups/cool-downs. A fit person can maintain moderate fitness at this intensity but won't see improvement.	Strengthens the heart and prepares the body for longer workouts and moving up to higher intensities. The body uses a high percentage of fat for fuel and body fat decreases. Gains in muscle mass also occur.
70–80% of Max HR	Become fitter, faster, and stronger without much risk of overtraining. Most recreational runners and serious athletes spend from 25 to 70 percent of their weekly training at this intensity.	Increases the size and strength of your heart. Improves your aerobic capacity and your cardiopulmonary (heart and lungs) fitness.
80–90% of Max HR	Train at or near your anaerobic threshold HR for better athletic performance. With two weekly workouts in this zone, you will see significant improvements in speed.	Moves anaerobic, threshold heart rate closer to Max HR. As this occurs you can perform better with less effort.
90–100% of Max HR	Prepare for peak athletic performance. The extremely fit can train here for short periods. Too much time in this zone can lead to overuse injuries, staleness, and cumulative fatigue.	Trains your fast-twitch muscles.

- Is genetically determined—you're born with it.
- Varies greatly among people of the same age.
- Is *not* an indicator of athletic ability.
- Is about the same for men and women.
- Cannot increase with training but can decrease from a sedentary lifestyle.
- Is sport-specific.
- Is affected by some drugs such as beta blockers.
- Remains fairly constant in fit individuals.

To estimate your Max HR, Anderson suggests that runners warm up easily for ten minutes then run eight hundred meters twice very hard with a one-minute jog between the two repeats. Your heart rate immediately after the second eight hundred meters is an estimate of your maximum.

Edwards developed a maximum heart rate protocol for fit individuals which requires only two to four minutes of really hard effort. This Max HR test is best performed on a track and requires the assistance of a partner who can run with you throughout the test, giving heart rate readings and setting a hard pace.

Maximum heart rate can also be determined by a physician or other health professional in a laboratory setting (called a maximal stress test). As a word of caution, talk to your own personal physician to determine which Max HR calculation or test is appropriate.

After completing a medically appropriate test and determining Max HR, you're ready to develop a training or fitness program around the heart rate zones which meet your current level of fitness and personal objectives.

How you use your monitor is determined by what you hope to accomplish. Remember, the body responds and adapts to different intensities of exercise. In heart zone training, these intensities are measured by actual heart rate, *not* speed or some level of perceived exertion.

The training terms and principles presented in chapter five are listed below, using heart rate as a guide. These percentages are

SALLY EDWARDS'S RUNNING
MAX HEART-RATE TEST

NOTE: Before taking this or any Max HR test, refer to the guidelines offered in chapter one and check with your personal physician.

Equipment:

- Runner testee wearing chest transmitter
- Runner partner wearing receiver with stopwatch set to zero
- Four hundred-meter track, running gear

Steps:

1. Testee and partner warm up by running two to six easy laps at 60 percent of mathematically calculated Max HR $(220-age) \times 0.60$.
2. At the starting point, the partner sets a gradually increasing pace. The goal is to reach Max HR in between two and four minutes.
3. Every fifteen seconds, partner announces testee's heart rate and elapsed time such as, "One minute, 155."
4. If testee reaches the three-minute mark without maxing, continue to accelerate, and try to reach max within sixty seconds.
5. At this point, testee is running extremely fast, can no longer talk, and is breathing rapidly and hard.
6. The partner should now be announcing heart rate every few seconds, yelling encouragement, and gradually accelerating until testee can no longer maintain form, speed, or willingness to run. The maximum is reached when the testee's heart rate no longer climbs.
7. The partner calls an end to the test.
8. Warm down with a slow walk to recover, then jog an easy two to six laps for total recovery.

reasonable comparisons for most experienced runners. Individuals who are new to exercise or running may need to use lower percentages until their aerobic fitness improves. Very fit, high-performance athletes, on the other hand, are usually able to train and race at consistently higher heart rates than most other folks. They may not become "anaerobic," for example, until reaching 90 percent of Max HR or even higher.

Training in Terms of Heart Rate

Easy	=	Less than 70 percent of Max HR
Comfortable	=	60 to 80 percent of Max HR
Long Slow Distance	=	Less than 75 percent of Max HR
Aerobic	=	Less than 80 percent of Max HR
Hard	=	Greater than 80 percent of Max HR
Anaerobic	=	Greater than 80 percent of Max HR
Tempo	=	About 85 percent of Max HR
Long intervals	=	90 to 95 percent of Max HR
Short or sprint intervals	=	95 to 100 percent of Max HR

Convert your current training schedule to heart rate training using simple math. To calculate the appropriate training zone or heart rate number for a particular workout, multiply the above percentages by your own Max HR.

For example, someone with a running Max HR of 200 bpm would do a tempo run by keeping their heart rate around 170 bpm as shown:

Maximum heart rate (200) × percentage (0.85) = tempo training heart rate (170)

HEARTFELT WORKOUTS

Most heart rate monitor books, several of which are listed in the appendix, offer comprehensive information on how to develop heart zone training and racing programs around your own goals

---

MONITOR TIP

The range of a heart monitor is about three feet or an arm's length. When two runners are both using monitors, interference can be minimized if each person wears his or her receiver on the "outside" wrist.

---

and current level of fitness. Here are three easy-to-follow heart rate workouts which have been adapted for runners of different abilities. They appeared initially in *The Fitness Monitor*, a bimonthly newsletter for heart rate monitor users. Although specific warm-ups and cool-downs are included within each workout, adapt their duration and intensity to meet your individual needs.

When Normal Heart Rate Isn't Normal

After using a monitor on a consistent basis, most runners and other athletes begin to recognize what heart rate numbers are "normal" for themselves during training, racing, rest, and recovery. Sudden or significant changes in heart rate may indicate a problem. Many different conditions can affect heart rate including

REST AND RECOVERY WORKOUT
(all abilities, 30 min.)

This workout is designed to help you maintain your current level of fitness and recover from strenuous training.

Time (Minutes)	Heart Rate (Percentage of Max HR)
0–5 Warm-up	55
5–10	60
10–15	70
15–20	60
20–25	70
25–30 Cool-down	55

AEROBIC WAVE WORKOUT
(intermediate, 45 min.)

This workout breaks the monotony of a training at a steady heart rate by gently "waving" the intensity up and down but keeping you aerobic. It can be shortened ten minutes by doing only two waves rather than three.

Time (Minutes)	Heart Rate (Percentage of Max HR)
0–5 Warm-up	50–60
5–10	Gradually increase to 80
10–15	Gradually increase to 70
15–20	Gradually increase to 80
20–25	Gradually increase to 70
25–30	Gradually increase to 80
35–40	Gradually increase to 70
35–45 Cool-down	Continue decrease to 60–50

CLIMBING THE LADDER WORKOUT
(advanced, 20 min.)

This interval workout makes your heart work harder with each step up the ladder. If you are accustomed to high-intensity training, go up the ladder two or three times before ending with a cool-down.

Time (Minutes)		Heart Rate
Cumulative Time	Step Time	(Percentage of Max HR)
0–5 Warm-up	5	50–60
5–9	4	60–70
9-12	3	70–80
12-14	2	80–90
14-15	1	90–100
15–20 Cool-down	5	50–60

environmental factors (such as temperature, terrain, and altitude), electronic interference (other monitor users or nonhuman sources of electrical impulses), and personal matters (illness, sleep disturbance, and stress).

Beware of Cardiac Drift

One of the most common effects, called "cardiac drift," appears during long runs and other endurance activities. It is characterized by a gradual increase in heart rate, which begins to occur after about an hour of exercise. This normal response results primarily from dehydration or loss of body fluids; as you become dehydrated from less fluid in the body, your heart has to work harder to supply the muscles with the same amount of blood. By staying properly hydrated to keep cardiac drift to a minimum, your running performances will be better.

Higher-than-normal heart rates during training and at rest are often a sign of overtraining. As you become fit, your resting heart rate will lower and you will be able to run faster with less effort. Resting heart rate is one of the key markers to alert athletes of overtraining or other latent medical conditions. If your resting heart rate is 5 bpm above normal, take the day off or train only at low intensities.

To determine your true resting heart rate, take it first thing in the morning after opening your eyes but before lifting your head off the pillow or putting your feet on the ground. Resting heart rate is not the same as *ambient* heart rate, the number of beats per minute your heart contracts when you are awake but in a sedentary and stationary position.

SHOPPING FOR AND CHOOSING A MONITOR

Regardless of the monitor functions you seek, be a conscientious consumer by studying available options and comparing prices of similar units. The monitor market is changing rapidly and retailers and manufacturers are always discounting older models as more sophisticated units become available.

If you're sincere about heart zone training, select a model with the most features you can afford. Inevitably, many users end up buying a second monitor during their first year because they want additional capabilities. Some of the most widely available features are described below.

Watch functions. These include time of day, date, and lap time, are especially popular with runners because most models eliminate the need for wearing both a monitor and sports watch. Typically, these dual-function monitors cost more than a heart rate-only model.

Programmable heart rate functions. This type of function allows you to set a specific workout zone. If your heart rate exceeds or drops below the set zone, the monitor lets you know by sounding an audio alarm or showing a visual indicator such as an arrow or blinking number. Some monitors allow you to program any zone, such as 143 to 152 bpm. Other monitors limit hi-low functions to five-beat increments such as 140 to 150 bpm or 145 to 155 bpm.

If you work out with other runners, consider buying a monitor which allows you to turn off the audio alarm. The beeping can become annoying to friends who don't share your enthusiasm for heart zone training or who are wearing their own monitors.

Memory functions. Useful to monitor users who want to do more than watch their heart rates during workouts. Memory functions allow you to recall certain heart readings after the workout is over. These readings will vary according to your specific monitor brand and model.

Recall functions. One common recall function will tell you how much time you spend in, over, and below your designated zone. Several upper-end models will also indicate your average heart rate. Some models allow you to specify the time increment to record, such as thirty seconds. At the end of the workout, you can then recall your recording and see your heart rate at the designated intervals.

QUICK FIXES

Here are a few simple solutions to some of the most common heart monitor problems. To extend the life of your monitor, always follow the manufacturer's instructions for care and use.

Dim or blank display on watch receiver Usually it's time for a new battery.

Constant moisture in watch receiver Have the gasket replaced and the unit pressure-tested.

Occasional fog in watch receiver Set it by a window (not in the sun) to dry out.

Heart rate jumps or spikes Adjust the chest band and look for electronic interference.

No heart rate signal Tighten the chest band to make it snug. Wipe the electrodes clean and wet them. Check the placement of the transmitter and its battery.

Heart rates over 200 bpm Usually caused by cross-talk from other users. Move at least an arm's length away or use a coded transmitter. Normal heart rates for a child often reach 200 bpm because they have smaller hearts and less total blood volume.

(Reprinted with permission of *The Fitness Monitor.*)

Stopwatch and lap features. By hitting the stopwatch or lap button during a run or race, you can go back later and see the individual lap times and corresponding heart rate.

Interval or pace alarms. These are frequently included on some of the higher-priced monitors. Many monitors with stopwatch features also include one or more alarms. Interval or pace alarms (which go off at set intervals, such as every two minutes) should not be confused with daily alarms (which go off at a certain time of day, such as 1 P.M.) or hi-low alarms (which go off according to a predetermined heart rate) found on some monitors. A word of caution: some alarms are louder than others. Most alarms, however, are hard to discern in noisy environments such as gyms and busy roads.

Water Resistant. Most but not all monitors are **water-resistant** and can be used for swimming or in inclement weather. If this feature is essential for your needs, review the warranty and use instructions carefully. Do not, under any circumstances, press monitor buttons under the water. This forces water into the unit and reduces its life. If you intend to swim with a monitor, remember that Max HR is sport-specific; the heart rate numbers for running will not be appropriate for swimming. In general, your swimming Max HR will be about ten bpm lower than for running.

Special Mounts. Many manufacturers also offer special mounts that allow you to use the monitor more efficiently on bicycles or other types of fitness equipment. Some monitors include mounts at no additional cost, while others charge extra.

Computer-related accessories and capabilities. Previously available only on very expensive units, are becoming more affordable and widely available. With some models you can use a computer interface unit and software to download recorded heart rate data for analysis and graphic display. A variety of software programs enable you to manually enter heart rate data, then incorporate the information into training programs and logs, to analyze it.

Keep in mind that all the features and functions on the market won't make your heart zone training effective unless you learn to use the monitor. Take the time to read the instruction manual from cover to cover at least once and practice using the buttons until you can program it easily.

RESOURCES

For more information on heart rate monitor training read:

Benson, Roy. *Precision Running with Your Polar Heart Rate Monitor.* Finland: Polar Electro Oy, 1994.

Edwards, Sally. *The Heart Rate Monitor Book*. Finland: Polar Eletro Oy, 1992.

————. *Heart Zone Training*. Boston, Mass.: Adams Media, 1996.

————. *Smart Heart*. Sacramento, Calif.: Heart Zones Company, 1997.

Parker, John L. *Heart Monitor Training for the Complete Idiot*. Tallahassee, Fla.: Cedarwinds Publishing, 1998.

For a free sample of *The Fitness Monitor,* a bimonthly heart rate monitor newsletter, send a self-addressed, stamped envelope to:

The *Fitness Monitor*/RS
2636 Fulton Ave., Suite 100
Sacramento, CA 95821

For dealer locations and information on specific models of wireless heart-rate monitors:

Acumen: www.acumeninc.com, 1-800-852-7823
Cardiosport: www.cardiosport.com, 1-888-760-3059
Freestyle: www.freestyleusa.com, 1-800-949-1563
New Life Technologies: www.newlifetech.com,
    1-800-NEW-LIF2
Polar: www.polar.fi, 1-800-290-6330
Sensor Dynamics: www.sensordynamics.com, 1-800-764-4327
Trek: 1-800-369-8735
Vetta: www.vetta.com, 1-800-GO-VETTA

CHAPTER TEN

Discussing Topics Runners Never Talk About

Running with the same training partners week after week, you get to know each other pretty well. After the first two or three miles of a run when you cover all the basics—the weather, work, and sports—the conversation usually turns to more personal matters like kids, money, relationships, and maybe even sex. What you won't usually hear about are some "unmentionable" concerns that affect countless runners everyday. They don't talk about their "leaking" problem or the gas or diarrhea experienced during every long run. Some runners may even suspect that their emaciated partner has a serious eating disorder but will remain silent on the matter.

These situations are probably more common than you think. Although some of the problems can be addressed with a little self-help, others will require the attention of a qualified health-care practitioner.

URINARY INCONTINENCE

Urine leakage or loss of bladder control is nothing to be ashamed about. It's a medical condition, known as urinary incontinence, which affects about 13 million Americans including 11 million women. According to one estimate, one in four women between the ages of thirty and fifty-nine have incontinence at one time or another. If urine "accidents" are hampering your enjoyment of running or is preventing you from participating in the sport, don't despair. The odds of improvement are excellent for those people who seek treatment.

Bladder problems are so widespread that the federal government and a group of professional and patient advocacy groups recently launched a public-health awareness campaign to educate people about the various symptoms, causes, and treatment options. As their educational materials point out, urine leakage isn't normal and nearly everyone with a bladder-control problem can be helped. For runners and others who leak urine when exercising vigorously, that's good news.

The most common type of bladder-control problem, known as stress incontinence, occurs when the muscles that keep your bladder closed are weak. Typically, these muscles stretch and weaken in pregnancy and childbirth or weaken at menopause when estrogen levels drop. Frequent constipation, heredity, and being overweight can also weaken the muscles. By toning the bladder-control muscles with pelvic or Kegel exercises, it is often possible to eliminate or reduce accidental leaking. If you aren't familiar with pelvic-muscle exercises, your gynecologist, urologist, or other health professional can explain how to do them correctly.

If the exercises don't help, a number of other treatments are available including electrical stimulation, biofeedback, medicines, and surgery. Your doctor can also tell you about special devices that don't cure bladder-control problems but can help prevent leakage. Remember that bladder-control problems don't have to be a normal part of living. Almost everyone can be helped so do seek treatment. In some cases, bladder problems are symptomatic of a more serious medical condition.

GASTROINTESTINAL PROBLEMS

Having diarrhea in the comfort of your own home is never any fun. Having it during a training run or race is a nightmare. The exact causes of frequent, loose bowel movements (known as the runner's trots) or other gastrointestinal (GI) problems (such as cramping, vomiting, gas, and heartburn) that occur during or immediately following a run or strenuous exercise vary from person to person. Certain foods, the timing of ingestion, caffeine, dehydration, and training intensity are some of the common culprits. Running appears to jar the colon and speed waste through the body. It also slows digestion because normal blood flow to the stomach is reduced. The higher the intensity of the exercise, the longer digestion will take.

If your problems are exercise-related and not caused by something more serious like infection or disease, changing the timing or content of your prerun meals may eliminate or reduce distress. For many people, coffee, dairy products, and high-fat, high-fiber, or high-sugar foods spell trouble. If problems only occur during races, improved conditioning, adequate hydration, and a timely bathroom visit may be the answer. A registered dietitian or sports nutritionist can make an individualized assessment and appropriate recommendations.

On a positive note, regular exercise is generally considered beneficial to the GI system. Studies even suggest regular physical activity may help prevent colon cancer. It takes time and experience, but most runners eventually identify and manage the source of any gut-wrenching problems.

NIPPLE BURN

Seeing a male runner with two bloody spots on the front of his shirt is disconcerting. You can't help but pity the poor runner who has to endure the discomfort of having his nipples rubbed raw. Nipple burn or "runner's nipple" is generally caused by the constant friction of damp, abrasive material against the nipple. It happens almost exclusively to men during long runs and races in warm weather. Nipple burn can usually be prevented in one of two ways: by protecting the nipples from friction or by eliminating the cause of friction.

Shirts with stitching, seams, or logos across the chest tend to be the most irritating along with cotton shirts that stay damp. If a shirt feels rough to the touch, it will probably chafe your nipples. Check your top to make sure it is smooth inside and select fabrics which are soft and wick moisture away from the body.

If you can't eliminate the source of friction (i.e., you want to wear the team shirt), consider using one of the commercial runner's lubricants designed to prevent chafing. For some people, plain old petroleum jelly is a cheap (albeit messy) way to protect the nipple. Adhesive patches, like those used on the feet, and adhesive tape also work well for runners who don't have much chest hair.

EATING DISORDERS

At any given time, approximately half the adult women and one-quarter of the adult men in the United States are dieting to control their weight. Our obsession with being thin along with extreme dieting can contribute to the development of eating disorders in individuals with underlying emotional problems or poor self-image.

According to the National Eating Disorders Organization (NEDO), one of the oldest eating-disorder groups in the country, any individual can develop an eating disorder and no single event or factor is the cause. Males and females and all social and economic classes, races, and intelligence levels, they say, are affected. Unfortunately, many women who participate in sports like running, where better performance is tied to body weight, are at increased risk.

Two primary eating disorders are anorexia nervosa and bulimia nervosa. Anorexia nervosa is described as self-starvation. An individual with anorexia nervosa typically has abnormally low body weight—15 to 25 percent below normal for their height—and various symptoms (abdominal pain, cold intolerance, amenorrhea, lethargy) yet does not recognize the danger of her physical state. Anorexic individuals see themselves as fat while appearing emaciated to the people around them.

Identifying someone with an eating disorder can often be difficult and few people will admit to having a problem. Some common warning signs of anorexia nervosa include:

- Intense fear of becoming obese.
- Distorted self-image.
- Excessive exercising despite fatigue.
- Unusual eating rituals like cutting food into little pieces.
- Wearing baggy clothes or lots of layers.

Bulimia is characterized by bingeing on large amounts of food followed by attempts to prevent it from turning into body fat. A variety of purging techniques are used by bulimics including vomiting, laxatives, water pills, and excessive exercise. While experiencing some of the same physical symptoms as those with anorexia, individuals with bulimia tend to be of average weight.

Warning signs of bulimia include:

- Preoccupation with food, diet, weight, and body fat.
- Consuming vast quantities of high-calorie foods.
- Swollen glands.
- Tooth decay or discoloration.

If you recognize signs or otherwise suspect your running partner or someone else in your life has an eating disorder, NEDO says it's important to intervene. Early detection of disordered eating habits is one of the most important factors in a successful recovery.

Share your concern with the person in a caring, nonjudgmental way and explain what behaviors you have observed. Be supportive and offer help but don't expect them to admit they have a problem. Never discuss weight and eating. Focus your concern on their health and well-being and suggest they seek appropriate physical and psychological assessment. There are a number of national and local nonprofit organizations and other groups that can provide information and guidance on how to handle eating disorders.

RESOURCES

For comprehensive information about the causes, symptoms, and treatment of incontinence:

**National Kidney and Urologic Diseases Information
   Clearinghouse**
3 Information Way
Bethesda, MD 20892-3580
Phone: 1-800-891-5388
Fax: (301) 907-8906
E-mail: nkudic@aerie.com

For a copy of *Female Triad: Amenorrhea, Eating Disorders, and Osteoporosis,* an ACSM public-education brochure, send a business-size, self-addressed, stamped envelope to:

Public Information
American College of Sports Medicine
PO Box 1440
Indianapolis, IN 46206-1440

For information or assistance regarding eating disorders contact:

American Anorexia/Bulimia Association
165 W. 46th St., Suite 1108
New York, NY 10036
Phone: (212) 575-6200

National Eating Disorders Organization
6655 S. Yale Ave.
Tulsa, OK 74136

Phone: (918) 481-4044
Fax: (918) 481-4076
Web site: www.laureate.com/nedo

Anorexia Nervosa and Related Eating Disorders (ANRED)
Box 5102
Eugene, OR 97405
Phone: (503) 344-1144

For extensive information and resources on eating disorders go to:

Something Fishy Website on Eating Disorders
www.something-fishy.org

For more information about the prevention and treatment of osteoporosis contact:

National Osteoporosis Foundation
1232 22nd St., N.W.
Washington, DC 20037-1292
Phone: (202) 223-2226
Web site: www.nof.org

CHAPTER ELEVEN

Running Through Life

In the early days of running, the typical images of a runner were all the same—young men. Today, running is a life-long activity. Runners come in all ages and sizes and they can be found in every stage of the life-span cycle—from conception, and in the womb of running moms, to death many miles later. Some even say the secret to longevity is running through life, not letting it pass you by.

RUNNING FOR TWO

"Congratulations, you're pregnant." After months (or years) of trying to have a baby, those words are music to your ears. But within minutes the euphoria begins to fade as the realization of having to make major lifestyle changes takes hold. You may wonder, "What about my running?"

First, consult with your gynecologist or obstetrician regarding exercise, running, and your individual pregnancy. If you still have unanswered questions or concerns, Melpomene Institute may be able to help.

Founded in 1982, this nonprofit, grass-roots organization helps women and girls of all ages to understand the link between physical activity and health, through research, publications, and education. The group adopted the name Melpomene in honor of a Greek woman who scandalized officials at the 1896 Olympics by running the marathon even after she was told women could not enter the race.

Although there is no hard scientific evidence that regular exercise improves the outcome of pregnancy, staying active can help reduce common discomforts such as backache and constipation.

Exercise during and after pregnancy also helps moms get back into shape after the baby is born.

Until fairly recently, the American College of Obstetricians and Gynecologists (ACOG) guidelines for pregnant women recommended a maximal exercise heart rate of 140 beats per minute (bpm). ACOG's approach, based largely on animal studies, was designed to prevent pregnancy complications that could occur as the result of elevated heart rates and increased body temperature during exercise.

In 1994, based on new research and the recognition that exercising at 140 bpm can show a wide variation in intensity from one pregnant woman to the next, ACOG updated its guidelines.

According to ACOG, no human data indicate that pregnant women should limit exercise intensity or lower training heart rates because of potential adverse effects. Therefore, ACOG now recommends that pregnant women who do not have any additional risk factors of adverse maternal or perinatal outcome can continue to exercise and will derive health benefits even from mild-to-moderate exercise routines.

Although a specific heart-rate limit is no longer specified, ACOG encourages pregnant women to modify the intensity of their exercise according to maternal symptoms. In their patient education pamphlet, *Exercise During Pregnancy,* ACOG makes the following recommendations:

1. *After twenty weeks* of pregnancy, avoid doing any exercises on your back.

2. *Avoid brisk exercise* in hot, humid weather or when you are sick with a fever.

3. *Wear comfortable clothing* that will help you to remain cool.

4. *Wear a bra that fits well* and gives lots of support to help protect your breasts.

5. *Drink plenty of water* to keep from overheating and dehydrating.

WARNING SIGNS

Pregnant women should also stop exercising when fatigued and not exercise to exhaustion. Additionally, stop exercising if you have any of the following symptoms during a workout and contact your doctor.

- Pain
- Dizziness
- Shortness of breath
- Feeling faint
- Vaginal bleeding
- Rapid heartbeat while resting
- Fluid leaking from the vagina
- Difficulty walking
- Contractions of the uterus
- No fetal movements

6. Consume the extra three hundred calories a day you need during pregnancy.

RUNNING AS A FAMILY ACTIVITY

When the U.S. Surgeon General released its 1996 report on physical activity and health, the statistics were alarming. A large segment of the adolescent and adult population do not achieve the recommended amount of regular physical activity. In fact, 25 percent of all adults are not active at all in their leisure time and nearly 15 percent of young people report no recent vigorous or light-to-moderate physical activity. Additionally, the report notes that daily enrollment in high school physical-education classes has dropped to 25 percent and physical activity declines dramatically with age during adolescence.

Increases in childhood obesity, largely the result of sedentary habits and high-fat diets, are of particular concern because many kids do not outgrow the problem. An estimated 40 percent of obese children become obese adults.

To counteract these unhealthy trends, the Centers for Disease Control and Prevention (CDC) subsequently released guidelines urging parents, schools, and communities to promote physical-activity programs for young people that will lead to lifelong benefits.

"Competitive sports are great, but they're not for all kids. On the other hand, physical activity is good for virtually everyone," says U.S. Department of Health and Human Services Secretary Donna E. Shalala.

The CDC notes that physical-activity promotion programs are likely to be effective when they:

- Emphasize enjoyable participation in lifelong physical activity.
- Offer a diverse range of competitive and noncompetitive activities that are appropriate for different ages and abilities.
- Develop student skills and confidence to participate in physical activity.
- Provide access to safe facilities outside of school hours.

Adults, as parents, teachers, and caregivers, play an important role in helping children develop healthy attitudes and behaviors. Your eating and exercise habits will affect all the youngsters around you—your own, the neighbor kids, and maybe even the kids who see you running down the street. It is only natural that running parents want to involve their children in their sport. The question is when, and at what level.

Emphasize Play

In planning family fitness activities, pay attention to the child's age, developmental and motor skills, and interests. "The emphasis for all children should be play," says preschool teacher Francis Pease, a runner and mother of three. "They need to be encouraged to have fun and be praised for their effort and participation, not the end

ONE FAMILY'S STORY

Burl Jones and Carole Hood had been runners for nearly twenty years when daughter Alison came along. She changed their running and other aspects of their life.

"Your lifestyle does change but running is something you can do with your child," Jones says. The couple found they had to be more organized and shift their usual running schedule. For fifteen years before the baby, Jones and Hood ran together in the early morning. Now they take turns going solo during the week so that their daughter can stay home and sleep. Hood also says the couple doesn't do as many races as in the past and tend to focus on short distances rather than marathons.

Jones and Hood were able to do much longer runs when Alison was an infant. "She'd just fall asleep in the stroller," Jones says. Now three-year-old Alison is entertained and content for about five miles. "But we can't call it a 'baby' stroller anymore," Hood adds. "It's a 'girl' stroller, because Alison says she's not a baby."

Having grown up around running and the outdoors, Alison is an active child who likes to run, ride her bike, and play. She participated in her first kids fun run at the age of two. "I got a medal," she boasts.

According to Jones and Hood, as parents they didn't have to introduce Alison to running because it's always been a part of her life. "They get interested on their own," Jones says. "You don't have to say anything."

result." Keep in mind, she says, that attention spans are short and a child's perception of fun is often very different than an adult's.

Pease suggests parents introduce running to children through modeling and shared experiences. "Don't assume your youngster is too young to learn your running vocabulary or understand the hows and whys of your adult play—running," she says. Concepts like "why we always bring our water bottles" and "how we stretch" can be explained in age-appropriate language, Pease adds. "You should also let your children make some of their own choices about exercise." After telling your child that the two of you are going to the track so Mommy can do her speed work, provide several choices. Do you want to play on the grass with your soccer ball or shall we bring your bicycle?

Pease also suggests that parents be creative in finding ways to involve children in their actual running and exercise workouts if they ask to be included. When your stroller-bound little one wants to get out and run, why not let the child push the stroller or do his or her "run" the last few blocks from home or up the driveway?

Running Risks and Kids

Although running is one of the safest forms of exercise for children, it is not without risks. In *Children Running: A Guide for Parents and Kids,* a twenty-page Road Runners Club of America brochure, parents are cautioned about several conditions that could expose a child to greater risks than other activities. They include:

1. *Any genetic defect* or congenital disease that might threaten the health of the child.

2. *Possible danger of injury* to the growth plates—the cartilaginous soft tissue—of the bones from too much stress too soon.

3. *Greater susceptibility* to heat injury.

Talking with your child's physician and listening to your child can minimize all of these risks. Children will tell you if something is too strenuous or if they want to stop the activity.

In the same publication, Gabe Mirkin says a more serious concern about early training is that an overemphasis on winning can cause children to hate exercise. "Children like to play. Replacing play with hard training can cause many children to stop exercising forever," he notes.

OVER FORTY BUT NOT OVER THE HILL

There was a time when middle age indicated that runners were over the hill and old age necessitated a transition from running to walking and rocking (as in chair). Fueled by the unfounded belief that significant declines in health and performance were an unavoidable result of aging, older runners were happy to just keep moving, albeit easier and slower. Generally speaking, they didn't set new running goals, maintain high-intensity training, or aspire to become better runners. And if you hadn't become a runner by around the age of forty, you wouldn't dare start running later in life.

Fortunately, those antiquated perspectives have changed. As long-time runner Richard Benyo notes in the preface of his book, *Running Past 50*, "There is growing evidence that Jack LaLanne's half-century old adage, 'Use it or lose it,' is firmly grounded in science."

In 1992, Ball State University released findings of the first longitudinal study to explore the effects of aging. The study began in the early 1970s, when researchers poked, prodded, and tested about three dozen male, elite-class, competitive runners including Frank Shorter, Jeff Galloway, and Amby Burfoot.

More than twenty years later, these same athletes were retested and divided into three groups: those who continued to train vigorously; those who became fitness runners; and those who became sedentary.

Results of "The Old Men Study" as it's become known, showed that athletes who continued to train vigorously had no loss of maximum heart rate, cardiovascular function ($VO_{2\,Max}$), or stride length even twenty years later. It seemed apparent that inactivity and disuse, not aging, are more likely causes of physiological decline.

More recently, the American College of Sports Medicine acknowledged a similar conclusion in its 1998 position stand,

"Exercise and Physical Activity for Older Adults." Participation in regular physical activity (both aerobic and strength exercises), ACSM says, is an effective way to reduce or prevent a number of functional declines associated with aging. Their pronouncement, which cited 248 references, also notes that during endurance exercise training, older adults elicit the same cardiovascular responses as young adults. Improvements occur as a function of training at higher intensity while light-intensity training results in minimal or no changes.

So what does this mean for older runners? In a nutshell, if you want to develop or maintain high levels of fitness you have to do some high-intensity training. Can your running continue to improve after middle age? It depends on factors including the age when you started running. Can improvements in health and fitness occur if you begin exercising after decades of being sedentary? Absolutely.

Normal, Healthy Aging

Normal aging is not without some undeniable physiological changes for runners and nonrunners. "Aging is a very complex process," says American College of Sports Medicine member Robert S. Mazzeo. "It involves a great many variables that interact with one another, but regular physical activity seems to cut across all of them and contribute to the physical and psychological well-being that defines healthy aging."

For the sedentary population, aerobic capacity, or the body's ability to take in and use oxygen, will decline up to 1 percent a year after the age of thirty. By continuing to exercise regularly you can cut that decline dramatically but you will still lose some aerobic capacity.

With age, flexibility also decreases as the muscles become less elastic and the range of motion becomes impaired. Aging also brings about declines in muscle strength and bone density. One

AGE-DEFYING INSPIRATIONS

Sister Marion Irvine, who gained notoriety as "the Running Nun" in the late 1970s, didn't let age hold her back. She took her first running step at forty-eight after thirty years of inactivity and a two-pack-a-day cigarette habit. At fifty-four she was the oldest competitor in the 1984 Olympic Marathon Trials having qualified for the event by running a 2:51:01 marathon. Despite having stopped racing a few years ago, the sixty-eight year old can still run circles around some men and women half her age.

Seventy-five-year-old runner Paul Reese is another example of age-defying inspiration. At seventy-three, the prostate cancer survivor crossed the United States on foot by running an average of 26.2 miles a day for 124 consecutive days. He then wrote about his cross-country experiences in *Ten Million Steps*. The book closes with Reese's own prescription for successful aging: "The secret to growing old is always having something to look forward to." Taking his own advice to heart, Reese subsequently ran across each of the fifty states and recounted those experiences in *Go East, Old Man*.

study indicated that by the age of seventy, the muscular system undergoes a 40 percent loss of muscle mass and a 30 percent decrease in strength. The lean-muscle decrease, body-fat increase, and decreased appetite associated with aging also cause the metabolism to slow.

Unfortunately, little can be done to change the genetically based declines but paying attention to lifestyle factors like disuse and poor nutrition can reduce the risk of illness and improve general fitness of even the very old and frail.

Regular weight-bearing activity (like running), strength or resistance training, stretching, and healthy eating will help slow, prevent, and sometimes reverse typical declines in health and fitness that come with aging and a sedentary lifestyle. Exercise has also been associated with more effective stress management, fewer sleep disorders, brighter mental outlook, less depression and anxiety, and reduced loneliness.

In *Running and Racing after 35,* authors Allan Lawrence and Mark Scheid caution runners that the combined physical effects of aging are not as devastating to athletes as the psychological effects.

"If you believe that you will slow down," they say, "you will slow down—that is a running truism no matter what your age!"

The good news for older runners is that they have something young runners can only dream about: the wisdom, confidence, and knowledge that comes from experience, which can be used to make each and every run and race the best it can be.

To stay healthy and keep running, older runners must train smarter, which often means allowing extra time for adequate rest and recovery. The late George Sheehan, a lifelong runner who is often called the "father of running," set a personal record in the marathon at sixty. This achievement occurred after making one significant change in his training schedule. He maintained his weekly mileage while gradually decreasing the frequency of his runs. By running every other day instead of every day, his body got the recovery it needed to rest, rebuild, and ultimately run faster.

RESOURCES

Women

For information of specific interest to women read:

Kowalchik, Claire. *The Complete Book of Running for Women.* New York: Simon & Schuster, 1999.

Samuelson, Joan Benoit and Gloria Averbuch. *Joan Samuelson's Running for Women.* Emmaus, Pa.: Rodale Press, 1995.

Switzer, Kathrine. *Running and Walking for Women Over 40: The Road to Sanity and Vanity.* New York: St. Martin's Griffin, 1998.

For information about educational programs, research, advocacy, and grants supporting the participation of women and girls in sports and fitness:

Women's Sports Foundation
Eisenhower Park
East Meadow, NY 11554
Information line: 1-800-227-3988
Phone: (516) 542-4700
Fax: (516) 542-4716
E-mail: wosport@aol.com
Web site: www.lifetimetv.com/WoSport

Melpomene Institute
1010 University Ave.
St. Paul, MN 55104
Phone: (651) 642-1951
Fax: (651) 642-1871
E-mail: melpomen@skypoint.com
Web site: www.melpomene.org

For more information on keeping active during pregnancy and other women's health issues read:

Butler, Joan Marie. *Fit & Pregnant: The Pregnant Woman's Guide to Exercise.* Waverly, N.Y.: Acorn Publishing, 1996.

Clapp, James F. III. *Exercising Through Your Pregnancy.* Champaign, Ill.: Human Kinetics, 1998.

Lutter, Judy Mahle and Lynn Jaffee. *The Bodywise Woman.* Champaign, Ill.: Human Kinetics, 1996.

Shangold, Mona and Gabe Mirkin. *Women and Exercise: Physiology and Sports Medicine.* F. A. Davis, 1994.

For a free copy of the pamphlet *Exercise and Pregnancy:*

American College of Obstetricians and Gynecologists
409 12th St., SW
Washington, DC 20024-2188

For on-line personal stories and other information about running during pregnancy, check the "Running on Full" forum under Fitness at: www.lifematters.com.

Children and Families

For more information on how to involve children in fitness and exercise read:

Kalish, Susan. *Your Child's Fitness: Practical Advice for Parents.* Champaign, Ill.: Human Kinetics, 1995.

For a twenty-page booklet, *Children's Running, a Guide for Parents and Kids,* send a two dollar check to:

Road Runners Club of America
1150 S. Washington St., #250
Alexandria, VA 22314
Phone: (703) 836-0558

RRCA also publishes a children's running curriculum guide for teachers and coaches (five dollars) and a twenty-five-minute children's running video (ten dollars).

For the ACSM fact sheet, Jogging Strollers, send a business-size, self-addressed, stamped envelope to:

Public Information
American College of Sports Medicine
PO Box 1440
Indianapolis, IN 46206-1440

To find out how fit your family is, send a self-addressed, stamped (55¢), business-size envelope and request the pamphlet *Fitness is a Family Affair*:

American Running and Fitness Association
4405 East West Hwy., Suite 405
Bethesda, MD 20814

For running stories and articles by and for kids plus a list of nonfiction and fiction running books for grades K–12, visit the Way Too Cool Kids Page at www.coolrunning.com.

Over Forty Runners

For more information about running after forty read:

Benyo, Richard. *Running Past 50: A Guide for Getting the Most Out of Your Running in the Second Half-Century of Your Life.* Champaign, Ill.: Human Kinetics, 1998.
Lawrence, Allan and Mark Scheid. *Running & Racing After 35.* New York: Little, Brown and Company, 1990.
Rodgers, Bill and Priscilla Welch with Joe Henderson. *Bill Rodgers and Priscilla Welch on Master Running and Racing for Runners Over 40.* Emmaus, Pa.: Rodale Press, 1991.

For a list of publications and free information on health and aging:

National Institute on Aging Information Center
PO Box 8057
Gaithersburg, MD 20898-8057
Phone: 1-800-222-2225 or (301) 496-1752

For information on *Mastersports,* a monthly newsletter dedicated to the over-forty athlete, call 1-800-562-1973.

To subscribe to *National Masters News,* a monthly publication for masters runners:

National Masters News
PO Box 50098
Eugene, OR 97405
Phone: (541) 343-7716
E-mail: suzy@nationalmastersnews.com
Web site: www.nationalmastersnews.com

To find local, regional, statewide, and national sports and fitness programs for men and women over fifty, see the Active & Ageless Resource Guide at: www.sportlink.com/hotlinks/active_ageless or send a seven dollar check to:

Active & Ageless Resource Guide
c/o Sporting Goods Manufacturers Association
200 Castlewood Dr.
North Palm Beach, FL 33408-5696
Phone: (561) 840-1150
Fax: (561) 840-1130

To help in research studies on "active aging" and learn more about exercise and fitness while aging:

Fifty Plus Fitness Association
PO Box D
Stanford, CA 94309
Phone: (650) 323-6160
Fax: (650) 323-6119
E-mail: fitness@ix.netcom.com
Web site: www.50plus.org

For a free copy of *Exercise: A Guide from the National Institute on Aging*, a one hundred-page publication with examples of recommended exercises, nutritional guides, and other information, contact:

Doralle Denenberg Segal
Office on Women's Health
U.S. Public Health Service
200 Independence Ave., SW, Room 730-B
Washington, DC 20201
Phone: (202) 260-9275
Fax: (202) 690-7172
E-mail: dsegal@sophs.dhhs.gov

CHAPTER TWELVE

Racing and Running Around

Some men and women enjoy a lifetime of running and never step up to a starting line. Competition, for them, holds no special appeal. For many other runners, racing gives exercise and running purpose. Races can mark special days for "putting the pedal to the metal" and testing their prowess against other competitors. Runners also use races to challenge the worthiest of opponents—me, myself, and I. And some runners just like the social aspect of meeting friends for a quick romp on a race course followed by a well-deserved mocha and bagel.

Running, unlike most competitive sports, offers equal-opportunity regardless of ability. With few exceptions (such as the Boston Marathon), anyone can enter and participate in the same races as world champions and Olympians.

FUN RUNS AND ROAD RACES ARE DIFFERENT

On any given weekend including most holidays, at least one road race or fun run will be offered in every metropolitan area throughout the United States. These events vary dramatically in terms of participants, course length, cost, and the amenities.

The primary difference between a fun run and a competitive race is the level of organization. Independent fun runs tend to be smaller and operate rather loosely: course length may not be certified as accurate, only ribbons may be awarded as prizes, and the aid station (if one exists) is a hose or sprinkler from somebody's yard.

Shorter fun runs or walks conducted in conjunction with longer competitive races, on the other hand, are typically well organized and operated by race management companies, running clubs, or organizations which use the events for fund-raising.

The United States of America Track and Field (USATF) is the national governing body for track-and-field and road-running events. Among other duties, they are responsible for regulations and guidelines for national competition.

Fun runs and competitive races each have positive aspects that appeal to runners for different reasons. Fun runs are often free, low-key events while races usually cost at least twenty dollars and offer a competitive atmosphere. Many runners like the glory of wearing T-shirts from big, popular races and being able to say they were there. At any large fun run or race, novice and slower runners can enjoy a feeling of being rather anonymous in the crowds of runners with various abilities. At large events, unlike small ones, they don't have to worry about running alone or finishing last because many untrained runners and nonrunners participate.

If someone tells you a particular race is "great" ask why. Every year thousands of people flock to megaraces like San Francisco's Bay to Breakers but some of them never return once they discover it's more of a walk with a big party and a giant traffic jam. Sometimes it's exactly that atmosphere that keeps runners going back year after year.

RACING: FREQUENTLY ASKED QUESTIONS

Q. How far is 5-K?
A. Races in the United States are measured in either miles or kilometers (K) depending on the distance. One K is equal to about 0.6214 mile so a 5-K race is about 3.1 miles.

To calculate kilometers multiply the number of miles by 1.609. To calculate miles, multiply the number of kilometers by 0.6214.

Q. Will I get lost?
A. Course markings (chalk and signage) and volunteers usually keep entrants on the right route but runners do get lost from time to time. Lead vehicles that make wrong turns sometimes lead even front-runners astray. If getting lost is a concern, review the course map in advance. If you don't receive one as part of your registration materials then look for a map in the staging area at the start.

Q. Can I walk?
A. Running races are foot races and the only requirement is to move under your own power. If you intend to walk the entire distance, register as a walker (if possible) and make sure you can meet any specified cut-off time. If you intend to take walk breaks while running, sign up as a runner.

Ultimately, you will be judged on how long it takes you to reach the finish line. Running races that offer concurrent racewalking events are designed for competitive racewalkers who know and abide by strict requirements. If you sign up for that category and don't use the accepted racewalking technique, you will be disqualified if spotted by a judge.

Q. Why do race registrations cost so much?
A. Many runners don't realize that races cost a lot more to stage than the entry fees cover. According to race director Doug Thurston, a typical local 10-K road race with 500 entrants and no frills or prize money costs about $11,750 or $23.50 per runner. With estimated revenues of $8,750 in entry fees and a $4,000 sponsorship, the race just breaks even.

"The next time you fill out your entry-fee check for a race, consider the fee a bargain," Thurston says. "If you were paying the true costs, the check would be a lot higher."

As a runner, you can help make races and fun runs in your community a continued success. Always register for the

(Continued)

events you participate in and make it a point to thank and support the sponsoring organizations. You can also help keep costs down by volunteering or donating in-kind services like printing and refreshments. There's always plenty of work to do before, during, and after a race. Call the contact phone number on the race entry form and offer your assistance. You will rarely be turned away.

Twelve Tips to Make Your First Road Race Enjoyable

If you've never entered a race before, following these tips can make it stress-free and fun.

1. *Register well in advance* of the race so you don't get left out. You'll be guaranteed an entry, usually save a few bucks, and simplify race management's job tremendously. (Race entry fees are rarely refunded.)

2. *Pick up your race packet and number* the day before the race, if possible. That's one less thing to do on race day.

3. *Read over all race materials* to verify location, starting time, parking, and any special instructions. You don't need surprises on race morning.

4. *Lay out your running shoes,* clothes, and other items the night before so something isn't forgotten. Use the "Checklist of Race Day Essentials" in this chapter as a guide and pin your number on the *front* of your shirt.

5. *Go to bed early* so that you wake up feeling rested.

6. *Eat and drink what you normally consume* before morning runs. This is not the time to test your body's ability to digest something new.

7. *Allow plenty of time to drive* to the start, park, and pick up your registration packet (if it wasn't available earlier).

CHECKLIST OF RACE-DAY ESSENTIALS

- Shirt or top with number pinned on front
- Shorts
- Running shoes (worn previously on at least one run of same length as the race)
- Socks
- Hat or visor and sunglasses
- Watch/heart monitor
- Special weather gear—gloves, old long-sleeved shirt (or other throwaway items to stay warm before the start), large plastic bag with holes for head and arms
- Toiletries (sunblock, lip protection, petroleum jelly)
- Water bottle
- Post-race clothing and towel
- Warm-up bag (if check-in station is provided)
- Personal identification, including an emergency contact who is not at the race, insurance info, and blood type
- Money

8. *If you know you'll need to use the bathroom* before the start, get in line early and always pick the line with the most men. The lines get longer as the starting time looms closer, and you may not get a turn behind a door.

9. *In short races like a 5-K,* warming up is essential for fast runners and helpful to anyone. If time allows, go for an easy jog and insert a couple of speed bursts. A warm-up shouldn't tire you out. Plan your time accordingly so that you hear the announcer call runners to the line.

10. *The starting lineup at any race* or fun run is based on ability. Don't even think about elbowing to the front. You'll run a better time (and avoid getting knocked down or run over) by moving to the edge and seeding yourself according to the pace you *know* you can run for the race distance. If no pace

signs are posted, assume the five-minute milers are toeing the line and the twelve- to fourteen-minute milers are in the back just ahead of the walkers and strollers. Check your watch as you cross the starting line if you want to pace yourself along the way.

11. *Listen carefully* to the starter's last-minute announcements. You won't know if the information is really important unless you hear it.

12. *Pace yourself* and hold a little something back during the first half. An all-out sprint off the starting line is not the best strategy for a first-time racer. Most runners find that an even pace or a negative-split pace (running the second half faster than the first half) is more effective in the end.

13. *Above all, have fun.* With each step you can revel in the joy of knowing the finish time for your first race is also a personal record or "PR" for that distance.

COMMON RUNNING EVENTS AND DISTANCES

Road Racing

Fun runs and road races can be almost any length but some distances are more common than others. Typical road-racing distances include: 5, 10, 12, and 15 kilometers and 5 miles, 10 miles, half marathon (13.1 miles), and marathon (26 miles, 385 yards). In most events, runners compete for awards or prize money, which are given according to finish time among all participants, or within specific age groups or categories. Found extensively throughout North America, road races are usually open to runners of all ages, levels of ability, and experience.

In large events, championships, and races with prize money, the nationally ranked runners are seeded in the front to give them the best opportunity for winning and setting records.

Marathons

There was a time when only the fastest and most experienced runners dared to race 26.2 miles. With the introduction of group marathon-training programs, many of which raise funds for charitable causes like leukemia and diabetes, the picture has changed. The very first race for many runners is now a marathon and they don't stop with just one. Marathoning has become a social and recreational experience—an excuse to travel with friends to a new city and have fun. There is even a club of runners—the 50 States & D.C. Club—whose goal is to run a marathon in every U.S. state and the District of Columbia.

Race directors are responding to the ever-growing numbers of marathoners, many of whom just want to cross the finish line and don't care how long it takes, by extending cutoff times and making their events more friendly to slower runners.

While there are a number of excellent books on marathon training (see the appendix), the support and camaraderie of a group training program makes the challenge of 26.2 miles much easier.

Ultra Races

Races longer than a marathon are generally known as "ultramarathons" or "ultras." These endurance events are run point-to-point on trails and semipaved roads, conducted on loop courses, or held on tracks. The most common ultra distances are 50 kilometers, 100 kilometers, 50 miles, and 100 miles. Some ultras are based on time, either hours or days, and the runner who covers the most miles wins. In addition to having enough physical endurance to keep moving for hours and hours, ultras require a great deal of mental strength.

The Western States 100-Mile Endurance Run, now in its twenty-sixth year, is considered one of the most challenging ultras

WHAT'S THE BIG DEAL ABOUT BOSTON?

The Boston Marathon is different from the hundreds of other marathons held each year. Not only is it the oldest marathon in the country (founded in 1897), entry in the event is limited to a select number of runners. Except for a few hundred participants who qualify by raising funds for various charities, the rest must complete a prior marathon within a certain time based on age and sex.

For age-group competitors who win awards at local races, the qualifying times are reasonable. For the running masses, Boston represents a dream. Recreational runners often aspire to run the Boston Marathon someday but many won't ever get there.

To qualify for Boston, which is held in mid-April, you must run a qualifying marathon sometime between January 1 of the year prior to the race and mid-March of the race year. The 1998 qualifying times, established by the Boston Athletic Association and listed below, may change in subsequent years.

Age	Men	Women
18–34	3:10	3:40
35–39	3:15	3:45
40–44	3:20	3:50
45–49	3:25	3:55
50–54	3:30	4:00
55–59	3:35	4:05
60–64	3:40	4:10
65–69	3:45	4:15
70 +	3:50	4:20

in the United States. Held in California's rugged Sierra Nevada, it is not unusual for runners to experience cold temperatures with snow *and* blistering heat in a twenty-four-hour period.

For safety reasons and time constraints, many ultra events have special entry requirements, restrict the number of participants, and disqualify runners who fail to meet progressive time limits along the course. Before embarking on an ultra, even a shorter one, you should complete at least one marathon and preferably more.

In *Marathon and Beyond*, ultramarathoner Jeff Hagan notes that "past marathon experience is a valuable asset that can be used to your advantage when you train for and run your first ultramarathon." As an experienced marathoner, he adds, you know how to train for a long race, stay hydrated, pace yourself, deal with "The Wall," and make your mind work for you, not against you.

Track Racing

Most track meets are geared predominately to high school, collegiate, and elite (top level) runners. If the idea of running fast and hard for short distances is something you'd like to try, enter an all-comers track meet. They're usually held during the summer months. Like fun runs, all-comers meets encourage participation and welcome all ages and abilities including novices. Typical running events range in length from fifty to five thousand meters.

RUNNING BY OTHER NAMES

Although running is a complete sport by itself, there are numerous competitive, social, and recreational events which involve running skills. Many of these events debuted in the 1970s as the health-and-fitness craze swept the nation. If you're looking for new ways to spice up your running, consider one of the following.

Triathlons and Multisport Events

Eppie's Great Race in Sacramento, California is believed to be the first triathlon. Restaurateur Eppie Johnson, an avid kayaker, founded the run/bike/kayak event in the early 1970s that bears his name.

In 1978, a slightly different type of multisport event debuted in Hawaii. Navy commander John Collins created the Ironman Triathlon, a triple-endurance event based on three existing long-distance races: the Waikiki Rough Water Swim (2.4 miles), the Around-Oahu Bike Race (112 miles), and the Honolulu Marathon (26.2 miles).

Today, triathlons are usually swim/bike/run. The distances vary, with the shorter versions known as sprint triathlons. For many triathletes the swimming leg is by far the most difficult, so runners who have swimming backgrounds are at a distinct advantage. Staff at most bike shops and running specialty stores can tell you if there is a "tri for fun," the triathlon equivalent of a fun run, in your area.

The eight-city Danskin Women's Triathlon series, which hosts free training clinics several months before each race, is a popular event for first-time female triathletes. Entrants of all levels of ability (professional athletes to inexperienced novices) are encouraged to participate and the finish line remains open until all the women cross.

Running biathlons and duathlons alternate running and one other sport, usually cycling. A biathlon has two legs—bike/run or run/bike while a duathlon has three legs—run/bike/run or bike/run/bike. Two-sport races aren't as common as triathlons but most offer runners a great opportunity for cross-training and quad-building. The Alcatraz Challenge starts with a 1.3-mile swim in San Francisco Bay and ends with a 12-K run to the Golden Gate Bridge.

Adventure Racing

After the birth of the grueling Hawaii Ironman Triathlon twenty-six years ago, it was only a matter of time before someone created an even greater athletic challenge requiring more diverse skills than running, biking, and swimming.

For sponsored athletes and individuals with time and money on their hands, adventure racing was the answer. These multiday, multievent races, which surfaced in the 1990s, offer (as the name implies) an adventure. In the Eco-Challenge, one of the better-known adventure races, five-person teams participate in a number of events in an exotic or challenging location like the mountains of Morocco. All team members must follow a course map they receive only twenty-four hours in advance and must finish the race together. If one member can't go on, the team is disqualified. Although there are scheduled stops for changing gear and sports, the teams must generally provide for their own needs.

Typically at least one leg in an adventure race involves some type of running. The 1995 Eco-Challenge, for example, was a 270-mile race involving bushwhacking, mountain biking, trail running, climbing, rafting, canoeing/portage, and horseback riding. Mini adventure races for the average Joe and Jane are now being introduced in some communities.

Ride-and-Tie Events

Introduced in 1970 as a competitive sport, ride and tie events combine cross-country running with horseback riding. Some of those involved in the sport call it the most challenging, exhilarating, and rewarding race three friends could ever do. Each ride and tie consists of two runners and a horse or mule, typically racing on a 10-to-40-mile, cross-country course.

At the start of a ride and tie race, one person begins riding and the other runs. At some point down the trail, the rider dismounts, ties the horse to a tree, and continues on foot. When the first runner reaches the horse, she mounts up and rides to meet or pass the partner in front. They continue this pattern of "riding and tying" as often as desired (six times is the minimum amount required by the rules) until all three team members cross the finish line. To assure the well-being of the equine partners during races, several mandatory veterinary checks are included.

If ride and tie events sound appealing, the Ride & Tie Association can help locate a partner or horse and enroll you in their mentor program. For a similar but different experience, ride and tie events using mountain bikes are popular in some parts of the country.

Snowshoe Racing

If the snow keeps you from running outdoors during the winter months, consider training and racing on snowshoes. No, you don't have to waddle around on heavy, wooden shoes. The advent of lightweight, asymmetrical, high-tech sport snowshoes in the early 1990s has made snowshoeing a lot like regular running and walking with a little more effort. You can even wear running shoes with the newer models and only minor changes in running technique are necessary.

For maximum efficiency while running on snowshoes, keep the feet close together and close to the ground. For a 10-K race on a packed surface, snowshoe running will add an extra two to three minutes per mile to your usual running time.

To find a snowshoe race, check with cross-country ski resorts or retailers who sell or rent sport snowshoes. In warm-weather areas, snowshoe races on sand are the latest fad. Only time will tell if "sandshoeing" holds much long-term appeal to runners.

Orienteering and Rogaining

Popular in Europe, Australia, and the United States, foot orienteering is a competitive and recreational sport for adults and children. Combining the physical effort of running or walking with the mental skills of navigation, orienteers use a map and (sometimes) a compass to cover a cross-country course as quickly as possible. Orienteering competitions typically offer a variety of courses, which present physical and navigational challenges for all levels of ability.

Rogaining, a team sport, is a twelve- or twenty-four-hour version of an "O-event." Using a central base camp as a place to eat and sleep or rest, teams of two to five members travel on foot, trying to reach as many checkpoints as possible in the allotted time.

Local O-clubs, which can be contacted through the United States Orienteering Federation, offer training and coaching. In addition to foot-O events, ski-O and bike-O events are also held.

Hashing

"Hashing" describes an utterly unique event involving running, orienteering (without the map and compass), and partying. The runners who participate in the sport are known as Hash House "harriers and harriettes" or the more generic "hashers" and have nicknames. Hash House Harriers form loosely organized groups which get together regularly for a run or "hash." "The drinking club with a running problem" is the hashers motto.

According to the International Harrier Association, hashing originated in 1938 in Malaysia when a group of British officials and expatriates formed a running social club of sorts. Their runs were based on the old English game of hares and hounds. One or two members, the "hares," would be given a head start to blaze a trail and drop shredded paper as the "scent." The harriers would then pursue the hare. At the end, the thirsty harriers would all celebrate with a beer.

After dying out during World War II, hashing reappeared and spread to the United States and other parts of the world. Today, there are thousands of Hash House Harrier clubs. Following chalk, flour, or paper trails through cities, towns, and their outskirts, hashers are always ready to party at the end with a diet soda, some water, or even a cold beer.

To have a good time and widen your circle of running friends, give hashing a try. There's probably a group nearby. Ask around at your local running club or check the Internet. Be prepared for an unparalleled running experience and don't wear new shoes!

RESOURCES

Road Racing and Fun Runs

To find road racing events and fun runs in your area, stop by your local running specialty store, or check any of the national and regional running magazines and Internet sites provided in the appendix.

Marathons

For information on national marathon training programs offered in many communities throughout the United States and Canada:

American Diabetes Association's Team Diabetes, 1-800-254-9255
Jeff Galloway's Training Program (U.S.), 1-800-200-2771
Jeff Galloway's Training Program (Canada), 1-800-419-2906
Arthritis Foundation Joints in Motion Training Team,
 1-800-464-6240
Leukemia Society's Team in Training, 1-800-482-TEAM

For an annual listing of the top U.S. marathons see the January issue of *Runner's World* magazine or visit Runner's World Online at www.runnersworld.com.

For descriptions, contact information, and details on various marathons in North America and throughout the world read:

Craythorn, Dennis and Rich Hanna. *The Ultimate Guide to Marathons.* Sacramento, Calif.: Marathon Publishers, 1998.

―――――. *The Ultimate Guide to International Marathons.*
Sacramento, Calif.: Marathon Publishers, 1998.

For information on qualifying for the Boston Marathon send a
self-addressed, stamped (55¢) envelope to:

Boston Athletic Association
PO Box 1999 (current year)
Boston, MA 07148

For information on the 50 States & D.C. Club:

50 States and D.C. Club
123 Astoria Rd.
Springfield, IL 62704
E-mail: rad50dc@family-net.net
Web site: www.flash.net/%7Erace26/50dc

Ultra Races

For more information on races that are thirty miles and longer go
to: Ultramarathon World at http://fox.nstn.ca/~dblaikie.

Hashing

To locate the nearest Hash House Harrier chapter go to: www.
harrier.org, www.kanzelmeyer.simplenet.com/hash, or www.half-mind.
com.

Triathlons and Multisports Events

Triathlon Federation USA
3595 E. Fountain Blvd., Suite F-1
Colorado Springs, CO 80910
Phone: 1-800-TRI-1USA or (719) 597-9090
Fax: (719) 597-2121
E-mail: usatriathlon@usatriathlon.org
Web site: www.usatriathlon.org

Ride and Tie

The Ride & Tie Association
Box 697
Foresthill, CA 95631
Phone: (530) 367-2525
Web site: www.rideandtie.org

Orienteering

Boga, Steven. *Orienteering: The Sport of Navigating with Map & Compass.* Mechanicsburg, Pa.: Stackpole Books, 1997.
Palmer, Peter. *The Complete Orienteering Manual.* England: Crowood Press Ltd., 1997.

For a free brochure that explains orienteering basics or to locate a local club contact:

United States Orienteering Federation
PO Box 1444
Forest Park, GA 30298
Phone: (404) 363-2110
Web site: www.us.orienteering.org

Snowshoeing

International Amateur Snowshoe Racing Federation
8 Beriault
Hull, Quebec
Canada J8X 1A1

For general information on snowshoeing, snowshoe running technique, and places to snowshoe read:

Edwards, Sally and Melissa McKenzie. *Snowshoeing.* Champaign, Ill.: Human Kinetics, 1995.

Appendix

Note: It is impossible to identify and mention all the running-related resources available. Inclusion or exclusion from *The Runner's Sourcebook* should not be considered an endorsement or lack of one. Every effort was made to ensure the information was accurate and up-to-date. For corrections or updated sites go to http://members.aol.com/bltfitness/book.htm. Send any changes or errors to bltfitness@aol.com.

RUNNING ORGANIZATIONS

American Running and Fitness Association
4405 East West Hwy., Suite 405
Bethesda, MD 20814
Phone: 1-800-776-ARFA
Fax: (301) 913-9520
E-mail: arfarun@aol.com
Web site: www.arfa.org

ARFA is a nonprofit educational organization of runners. With its sister organization, the American Medical Athletic Association, ARFA promotes health and physical fitness among all ages through various programs and services. They publish *Running and FitNews,* a monthly newsletter for members.

Road Runners Club of America
1150 S. Washington St., Suite 250
Alexandria, VA 22314-4493
Phone: (703) 836-0558
Fax: (703) 836-4430

E-mail: office@rrca.org

Web site: www.rrca.org

RRCA promotes running as a competitive sport and healthful exercise through its 630 clubs and 180,000 members. The tax-exempt organization provides a wide range of resources, programs, and services to clubs and individual members. *Footnotes* is the quarterly magazine for members of RRCA clubs.

USA Track & Field
1 RCA Dome, Suite 140
Indianapolis, IN 46225
Phone: (317) 261-0500
Fax: (317) 261-0481
Web site: www.usatf.org

Road Running Information Center (RRIC)
5522 Camino Cerralvo
Santa Barbara, CA 93111
Phone: (805) 683-5868
Fax: (805) 967-5958
E-mail: honikman@silcom.com
Web site: www.usaldr.org

USAT&F is the national governing body for track-and-field, racewalking, and road-racing events including the marathon. *On the Roads* is their quarterly publication for members. RRIC, a USAT&F service, maintains running records, statistics, and other information on distance running and USAT&F.

RESOURCES FOR SHOES, APPAREL, RACE INFORMATION, ETC.

Alabama

College Street Sports
125 S. College St.
Auburn, AL 36830

Trac Shak
2915 Crescent Ave.
Birmingham, AL 35253

Alaska
Ridge Runners
564 E. Pioneer Ave.
Homer, AK 99603

Arizona
Runner's Den
6505 N. 16th St.
Phoenix, AZ 85016

Running Shop
3055 North Campbell
Tucson, AZ 85719

California
Fleet Feet Sports
26 Rancho Del Mar
Aptos, CA 95003

Fleet Feet Sports
222 W. 3rd St.
Chico, CA 95926

Fleet Feet Sports
515 Second St.
Davis, CA 95616

Fleet Feet Sports
2222 Francisco Dr.
El Dorado Hills, CA 95762

Phidippides-Encino
16545 Ventura Blvd.
Encino, CA 91436

Fleet Feet Sports
8128 Madison Ave.
Fair Oaks, CA 95628

A Snail's Pace
8780 Warner Ave.
Fountain Valley, CA 92708

A Snail's Pace
24741 Alicia Pl.
Laguna Hills, CA 92653

Runner's High
5463 East Carson
Long Beach, CA 90808

The Runner's High
859 Santa Cruz Ave.
Menlo Park, CA 94025

Fleet Feet Sports
310C Main St.
Pleasanton, CA 94566

Fleet Feet Sports
1850 Douglas Blvd.
Roseville, CA 95661

Fleet Feet Sports
2311 J St.
Sacramento, CA 95816

Fleet Feet Sports
2086 Chestnut St.
San Francisco, CA 94123

Hoy's Sports
1632 Haight St.
San Francisco, CA 94117

Fleet Feet Sports
643 Fourth St.
Santa Rosa, CA 95404

Athlete's Edge
437 S. Hwy. 101
Solano Beach, CA 92075

Inside Track
1410 E. Main St.
Ventura, CA 93001

Fleet Feet Sports
1528 Bonanza St.
Walnut Creek, CA 94596

Colorado

Boulder Running Company
2775 Pearl St.
Boulder, CO 80302

Runner's Roost
1129 Pearl St.
Boulder, CO 80304

Runner's Roost
1685 S. Colorado Blvd.
Denver, CO 80222

Mongoose Runners Den
8877 Harlan St.
Westminster, CO 80030-2930

Connecticut

Fleet Feet for Women
1003 B Farmington Ave.
Hartford, CT 06107

The Run In
2172 Silas Deane Hwy.
Rocky Hill, CT 06067

District of Columbia

Fleet Feet Sports
1841 Columbia Rd., NW
Washington, DC 20009

Florida

The Runner's Edge
3333 North Federal Hwy.
Boca Raton, FL 33431

Running Wild
5437 North Federal Hwy.
Ft. Lauderdale, FL 33308

Naples on the Run
2128 Ninth St., N
Naples, FL 34102

Track Shack
1322 North Mills Ave.
Orlando, FL 32803

FootWorks
5724 Sunset Dr.
South Miami, FL 33143

Georgia

Fleet Feet Sports
6221-A Roswell Rd.
Atlanta, GA 30328

Phidippides
220 Sandy Springs Cr.
Atlanta, GA 30328

Phidippides
Ansley Mall
1544 Piedmont Rd., NE
Atlanta, GA 30328

Hawaii

The Running Room
819 Kapuhula Ave.
Honolulu, HI 96816

Idaho

Bandanna Running and Walking
121 North St.
Boise, ID 83702

Illinois

Fleet Feet Sports
241-243 W. North Ave.
Chicago, IL 60610

Springfield Running Center
2943 W. White Oak Dr.
Springfield, IL 62704

Runner's Edge
1211 Wilmette Ave.
Wilmette, IL 60091

Indiana

Runners Forum
2454 E. 116th St.
Carmel, IN 46032

Athletic Annex Running Centre
1411 W. 86th St.
Indianapolis, IN 46260

Iowa

Running Wild
313 E. George Washington
Davenport, IA 52803

Kansas

Garry Gribble's Running Sports
Stoll Park Center
11932 W. 119th St.
Overland Park, KS 66213

Kentucky

John's Running Shop
317 S. Ashland
Lexington, KY 40502

Ken Combs Running Shop
4137 Shelbyville Rd.
Louisville, KY 40207

Louisiana

Phidippides
6601 Veterans Blvd.
Metairie, LA 70003

Southern Runner
6112 Magazine St.
New Orleans, LA 70118

Maryland

Racquet & Jog
4959 Elm St.
Bethesda, MD 20814

Feet First
10451 Twin River Rd.
Wildelake Village Green
Columbia, MD 21044

Massachusetts

Bill Rodgers Running Center
353-T N. Market Pl.
Boston, MA 32103

Runner's Edge
401 Main St.
Melrose, MA 02176

Runner's Shop
114 Main St.
Northampton, MA 01060

Yankee Runner
49 Pleasant St.
Newburyport, MA 01583

Michigan

Tortoise and Hare
209 E. Liberty St.
Ann Arbor, MI 48104

Bauman's Running Center
1453 West Hill Rd.
Flint, MI 48507

Complete Runner
915 S. Dort Hwy.
Flint, MI 48503

Gazelle Sports
3987 28th St.
Grand Rapids, MI 49512

Hanson's Running Shop
20641 Mack Ave.
Gross Pointe, MI 48236

Step One Running
2621 Wildwood Ave.
Jackson, MI 48503

Running Fit
151 E. Main
Northville, MI 48167

Total Runner
29207 Northwestern Hwy.
Southfield, MI 48034

Minnesota

Marathon Sports Ltd.
2304 W. 50th St.
Minneapolis, MN 55410

Runner's Edge
794 Grand Ave.
St. Paul, MN 55106

Run 'N Fun
868 Randolph Ave.
St. Paul, MN 55102

Mississippi

Phidippides Sports
1459 Jacksonia Plaza
Jackson, MS 39211

Missouri

Garry Gribble's Running Sports
Ward Parkway Mall
86700 Ward Pkwy.
Kansas City, MO 64114

Fleet Feet Sports
3899 S. Service Rd., #F
St. Peters, MO 63376

Nebraska

Walk N Run Fitness
519 78th St.
Omaha, NE 68114

Nevada

Fleet Feet
3807 S. Carson St.
Carson City, NV 89701

Fleet Feet Sports
2121 W. Williams St.
Fallon, NV 89406

New Hampshire

Runner's Alley
104 Congress St.
Portsmouth, NH 03801

New Jersey

Haddonfield Running Co.
144 Kings Hwy. E.
Haddonfield, NJ 08033

Fleet Feet Sports
Marlton Crossing Shopping Center
109 Route 73 S.
Marlton, NJ 08053

Fleet Feet Sports
603 Bloomfield Ave.
Monclair, NJ 07042

New Mexico

Gil's Runners Shoe World
3515 Lomas Blvd., NE
Alburquerque, NM 87106

Fleet Feet Sports
8238 Menaul Blvd., NE
Albuquerque, NM 87110

New York

The Running Start
2113 Avenue U
Brooklyn, NY 11229

Runner's Edge
294 Main St.
Farmingdale, NY 11735

Super Runners Shop
355 New York Ave.
Huntington, NY 11743

Paragon Sports
867 Broadway
New York, NY 10003

Super Runner's Shop
416 Third Ave.
New York, NY 10016

Gubbins Running Ahead
32 Windmill Ln.
Southhampton, NY 11968

North Carolina

Fleet Feet Sports
102-A E. Main St.
Carrboro, NC 27510

Run for Your Life
1412 East Blvd.
Charlotte, NC 28203

Phidippides Sports Center
Carolina Mall
Highway 29-N
Concord, NC 28025

Ohio

Runner's Supply Shop
3255 Cleveland Ave., NW
Canton, OH 44709

Fasttrack
138 the Arcade
401 Euclid Ave.
Cleveland, OH 44114

Ron Roncker's Running Spot
1993 Madison Rd.
Cincinnati, OH 45208

FrontRunner
1344 W. Lane Ave.
Columbus, OH 43221

Dave's Running Shop
203 Main St.
Delaware, OH 43515

Dave's Performance Footgear
5577 Monroe St.
Sylvania, OH 43560

Big Orange Shoe Shop
103 W. Baird St.
West Liberty, OH 43357

Jock Stop
7373 Market St.
Youngstown, OH 44512

Oregon

Run Pro
525 High St.
Eugene, OR 97401

Finish Line Sports
333 S. State St.
Lake Oswego, OR 97034

Pace Setter Athletics
4306 S.W. Woodstock
Portland, OR 97206

Pennsylvania

Bryn Mawr Running Co.
828 W. Lancaster Ave.
Bryn Mawr, PA 19010

Flying Feet Sports Shoes
1511 Mt. Rose Ave.
York, PA 17403

South Carolina

The Extra Mile
4711 Forest Dr., Suite 18
Columbia, SC 29206

Strictly Running
736 Harden St.
Columbia, SC 29205

South Dakota

Runner's Shop
615 Mount Rushmore Rd.
Rapid City, SD 57701-2752

Tennessee

Runners Market
4443 Kingston Pike
Knoxville, TN 37919

Fleet Feet Sports
597 Erin Dr.
Memphis, TN 38117

Texas

Run Tex
919 W. 12th St.
Austin, TX 78703

Fleet Feet Sports
514 Everhart Rd.
Corpus Christi, TX 78411

Luke's Locker
3607 Oak Lawn
Dallas, TX 75219

Fleet Feet Sports
2408 Rice Blvd.
Houston, TX 77005

Fleet Feet Sports
6586 Woodway
Houston, TX 77057

Fleet Feet Sports
6408 N. New Braunfels Ave.
San Antonio, TX 78209

Utah

DeBoer's Running Store
Five Points Mall
1614 S. Main St.
Bountiful, UT 84010

Salt Lake Running Co.
3130 Highland Dr.
Salt Lake City, UT 84106

Rob's Running Center
University Mall
Orem, UT 84097

Virginia

Pacers
1301 King St.
Alexandria, VA 22314

Fleet Feet Sports
7516 Leesburg Pike
Falls Church, VA 22043

Footsteps of Reston
11130 S. Lakes Dr., Suite H
Reston, VA 22091

Fleet Feet Sports
6119B Backlick Rd.
Springfield, VA 22150

Washington

Fast Lady Sports
5 Lake St.
Kirkland, WA 98033

Fast Lady Sports
7501 166th Ave., NE
Redmond, WA 98033

Super Jock 'N Jill
7210 E. Greenlake Dr.
Seattle, WA 98115

Fast Lady Sports
2710 N.E. University Village
Seattle, WA 98105

West Virginia

On the Run
3330 Emerson
Parkersburg, WV 26104

Hole N' Run
46 Washington Ave.
Wheeling, WV 26003

Mail Order Companies

California Best, 1-800-225-2378
RaceReady, 1-800-537-6868
Road Runner Sports, 1-800-551-5558
Tele-a-Runner, 1-800-835-2786
Title Nine Sports, 1-800-609-0092

MAGAZINES AND PUBLICATIONS
National

American Runner (seven issues/year)
137 Clinton Ave.
New Rochelle, NY 10801

Marathon and Beyond (bimonthly)
c/o Human Kinetics
PO Box 5076
Champaign, IL 61825-5076
Phone: 1-800-747-4457 (USA) or 1-800-465-7301 (Canada)
Fax: (217) 351-1549 (USA) or (519) 971-9797 (Canada)
Web site: www.humankinetics.com

Runner's World (monthly)
c/o Rodale Press
33 E. Minor St.
Emmaus, PA 18098
Phone: (610) 967-5171
Fax: (610) 967-8962
E-mail: rodaleDM@aol.com
Web site: www.runnersworld.com or www.rodalepress.com

Running Times (ten issues/year)
c/o Fitness Publishing, Inc.
98 N. Washington St.
Boston, MA 02114
Phone: (617) 367-2228
Fax: (617) 376-2350
E-mail: gordRTimes@aol.com

Youth Runner (quarterly)
PO Box 1156
Lake Oswego, OR 97035

Phone: (503) 236-2524
E-mail: Dank@YouthRunner.com
Web site: www.youthrunner.com
Circulation: Athletes 8–18 that compete in track, cross country, and
  road racing

Ultra Running (ten issues/year)
PO Box 400
Lee, MA 01238-0400
Phone: 1-888-858-7203 or (413) 243-0101
E-mail: dimac@javanet.com
Web site: www.ultrarunning.com

Local and Regional

Illinois Runner
PO Box 53
Fairbury, IL 61739

Indiana Running and Racing News
503 E. Main St.
Hartford City, IN 47348

The Indiana Runner (monthly)
Fit Press Inc.
PO Box 478
Shelbyville, IN 46176

Mainely Running (monthly)
2 Howards Hill Rd.
Brunswick, ME 04011

New Hampshire Runners (bimonthly)
PO Box 25
Newport, NH 03773

RacePlace (bimonthly)
16888 Saint Andrews Dr.
Poway, CA 92064
Phone: (619) 485-9806
Fax: (916) 485-9805
E-mail: rose@raceplace.com
Web site: www.raceplace.com
Circulation: Southern California

RacePlace Hawaii (quarterly)
4224 Waialea Ave., Suite 5-385
Honolulu, HI 96816
Phone/Fax: (808) 734-2204
E-mail: jedens@aloha.net

Runner's Gazette (monthly)
566 Fairfield Rd.
Lewisburg, PA 17837
Phone: (570) 524-9713
E-mail: RunGazette@aol.com
Circulation: Pennsylvania, Maryland, Delaware, Virginia,
    New Jersey, New York, West Virginia, and D.C.

Running Arkansas (monthly)
PO Box 91
Camden, AR 71701

S.W.E.A.T. Southwest Exercise and Training
5743 E. Thomas Rd., Suite 2
Scottsdale, AZ 85251
Phone: (602) 947-3900
Fax: (602) 947-1215

The Schedule (monthly except November/December)
80 Mitchell Blvd.
San Rafael, CA 94903

Phone: 1-800-998-7904 or (415) 472-7223
Fax: (415) 472-7233
E-mail: Editor@TheSchedule.com
Web site: www.Theschedule.com
Circulation: California

The Utah Runner and Cyclist (seven issues/year)
PO Box 58344
Salt Lake City, UT 84158-0344

The Running Network

Contact the following national and regional running magazines directly or through The Running Network, 833 Eastwind Dr., Westerville, OH 43081, www.runningnetwork.com. The Running Network is a marketing organization and clearinghouse for regional and specialized running magazines.

American Track & Field and *American Track & Field Athlete*
Shooting Start Media, Inc.
853 D'Onofrio Dr., Suite 203
Madison, WI 53719
Phone: (608) 827-0806
Fax: (608) 827-0811
E-mail: stanederjr@aol.com
Web site: www.runningnetwork.com/atf

California Track & Running News
Shooting Start Media, Inc.
853 D'Onofrio Dr., Suite 203
Madison, WI 53719
Phone: (608) 827-0806
Fax: (608) 827-0811
E-mail: stanederjr@aol.com
Web site: www.runningnetwork.com/CTRN

Chicago's Amateur Athlete (8 issues/year)
Chicago Sports Media, Inc.
7840 N. Lincoln Ave., Suite 208
Skokie, IL 60077
Phone: (847) 675-0200
Fax: (847) 675-2903
E-mail: run@chicagoaa.com
Web site: www.chicagoaa.com

Florida Running & Triathlon
8640 Tansy Dr.
Orlando, FL 32819-4529
Phone: (407) 352-9131
Fax: (407) 351-0191
E-mail: quetez@aol.com
Web site: www.runningnetwork.com/FloridaRunning

Hawaii Race
3442 Waialae Ave., Suite 6
Honolulu, HI 96816
Phone/Fax: (808) 922-4222
E-mail: mjaffe@aloha.net

Inside Texas Running (ten issues/year)
9514 Bristlebrook Dr.
Houston, TX 77083
Phone: (281) 498-3208
Fax: (281) 879-9980
Web site: www.runningnetwork.com/TexasRunning

Michigan Runner
9973 E. Grand River
Brighton, MI 48116
Phone: (810) 227-4200
E-mail: info@glsp.com

Midwest Runner
c/o New Voice Communications
217 N. Dunn
Bloomington, IN 47408
Phone: (812) 337-3311
Fax: (812) 337-3314
E-mail: beraig@new_voice.com

Missouri Runner
1105 Dogwood St.
Jefferson City, MO 65109
E-mail: editor@morunner.com

New England Runner
PO Box 1455
Brookline, MA 02446
Phone: (617) 232-8778
Fax: (617) 232-8772
E-mail: nerunner@ix.netcom.com
Web site: www.runningnetwork.com/NERunner

New York Runner
9 E. 89th St.
New York, NY 10128
Phone: (212) 860-4455, Ext. 243
Fax: (212) 860-9754

Northwest Runner
4831 N.E. 44th St.
Seattle, WA 98105
Phone: (206) 527-5301
Fax: (206) 527-1223
E-mail: nwrunner!@aa.net
Web site: www.runningnetwork.com/NWRunner

Oklahoma Runner & Triathlete
PO Box 2008
Tulsa, OK 74101-2008
Phone: (918) 581-8306
Fax: (918) 582-0415
E-mail: okrunjoe@webzone.net
Web site: www.runningnetwork.com/OKRunner

Race Center Northwest (six issues/year)
AA Sports Limited
4840 S.W. Western Ave., Suite 400
Beaverton, OR 97005
Phone: (503) 644-6822
Fax: (503) 520-0242
E-mail: aasports@racecenter.com
Web site: www.racecenter.com
Circulation: Oregon

Runner Triathlete News (monthly)
PO Box 19909
Houston, TX 77224
Phone: (713) 781-7090
Fax: (713) 781-9594
E-mail: rtnews@ix.netcom.com
Web site: runningnetwork.com/RunTriNews
Circulation: Texas, Louisiana, Arkansas, New Mexico, and
  Oklahoma

Running Journal (monthly)
PO Box 157
Greenville, TN 37743
Phone: (423) 638-4177
Fax: (423) 638-3328
E-mail: rj@xtn.net
Web site: www.runningnetwork.com/RunningJournal
Circulation: Alabama, Arkansas, Florida, Georgia, Kentucky,

Louisiana, Mississippi, North Carolina, South Carolina,
Tennessee, Virginia, West Virginia, Washington, D.C.,
and Maryland

RUNOHIO
PO Box 238
Granville, OH 43023
Phone: (740) 587-0376
Web site: www.runningnetwork.com/Ohio
Circulation: Ohio, West Virginia, and Northern Kentucky

Southern Runner
6112 Magazine St.
New Orleans, LA 70118
Phone: (504) 899-3333
Fax: (504) 885-4325
Circulation: Louisiana, Alabama, Mississippi, Florida, and Texas

Tailwinds
630 N. Craycroft Rd., Suite 141
Tucson, AZ 85711
Phone: (520) 745-2003
Fax: (520) 745-1992
E-mail: tailwind@dakotacom.net
Circulation: Arizona, Utah, Colorado, Southern California,
  and Nevada

Washington Running Report (six issues/year)
Capital Running Company
13710 Ashby Rd.
Rockville, MD 20853-2903
Phone: (301) 871-0005
Fax: (301) 871-0006
E-mail: runkathy@ix.netcom.com
Web site: www.runwashington.com
Circulation: Washington/Baltimore metro area extending
  throughout Maryland and Virginia

Newsletters

Peak Running Performance (six issues/year)
6150 Nancy Ridge Dr.
San Diego, CA 92121
Phone: 1-888-PEAKRUN
E-mail: contact@peakrun.com
Web site: www.peakrun.com

Running Commentary by Joe Henderson (monthly)
61 W. 34th Ave.
Eugene, OR 97405
Fax: (541) 344-9956
E-mail: joe@joehenderson.com
Web site: www.joehenderson.com

Running Research News (ten issues/year)
PO Box 27041
Lansing, MI 48909
Phone: (517) 371-4897
Fax: (517) 371-4447
E-mail: rrn@gisd.com
Web site: www.rrnews.com

teamPenguin News (monthly)
2005 Avenue of the Trees
Carlsbad, CA 92008
Phone: 1-800-254-9721
Web site: www.waddle-on.com

RUNNING ON-LINE AND THROUGH THE NET

With a wealth of information available on the Internet, you can run
from site to site to:

• Obtain training information.
• Find race schedules and course maps.

- Register for races and other events.
- Look up running statistics and race results.
- Self-diagnose and treat your aches and pains.
- Shop for shoes, running gear, and books.
- Identify good places to run around the United States and abroad.
- Discuss running topics with runners and others.
- Read running and fitness articles on-line.
- Locate a running club, training partner, or coach.
- Subscribe to running publications and mailing lists.

Cyberspace is still virtually unchecked; it is your responsibility to determine whether a site is legitimate. As you run through the net ask yourself three questions:

1. Who am I running with?

Always review each site to determine the source and sponsor of the information. Some of the best information comes from colleges and universities, professional associations, government agencies, and foundations. Some commercial sites have good information, but beware of biases. To be safe, pay attention to the suffixes at the end of a Web address:

- .com is a commercial account
- .edu is a school, college, or university
- .gov is a government agency
- .net is a community network or large organization
- .org is usually a nonprofit organization

2. Where am I running?

It takes only a quick tap of a button or click on the mouse to send you off and running to another site (sometimes without even knowing it). Through the use of off-site links you may actually end up someplace questionable even though you started out at a seemingly reliable site. If no telephone numbers or postal addresses are provided use caution in ordering merchandise and giving personal information.

3. Am I running up to speed?

Web sites and home pages come, go, and change very quickly. Always check to see when a site was updated so you'll know whether the information is current.

It's impossible to list even a fraction of the running sites on the World Wide Web. In addition to the many Web sites at the end of this chapter, the following addresses offer extensive running information and/or links to other informative and useful running-related sites.

Cool Running: www.coolrunning.com. A comprehensive site with lots of race results and great running pages for kids.

Dead Runner's Society: http://storm.cadcam.iupui.edu/drs/drs.html. An informal e-mail-based discussion group for people who like to talk about running and often meet at races.

GBTC Running Resouces: www.gbtc.org/whatelse. The Greater Boston Track Club Web site includes tons of links to clubs, commercial businesses, and just about anything of interest to a runner.

International Front Runners: www.frontrunners.org. Running clubs, calendar of events, forum, and other information of interest to gay and lesbian runners.

On the Run: www.ontherun.com. A Web magazine with general running resources and information of particular interest to runners in the Northwest.

Runner's World Online: www.runnersworld.com. This Web site by *Runner's World* magazine is a good first stop for a full range of reliable and timely information.

Running Amuck: www.fix.net/~doogie/links2.html. Offers hundreds of local, national, and international links to running-related organizations, resources, merchandise, and services.

Running Page: www.runningpage.com. Includes products, race info, clubs, and more.

Running Room: www.runningroom.com. An informative commercial site with many North American links.

Run the Planet: www.runtheplanet.com. Managed by the publishing house of *Podismo*, the Italian running magazine, this site describes places to run and walk throughout the United States and the world. Also features links to "weird running" sites such as nude running events, retrorunning (running backward), and costumed running.

The Runner's Web: www.runnersweb.com/running.html. A comprehensive Canadian site with lots of U.S. links including more than seventy interactive tools and calculators.

Human Kinetics: www.humankinetics.com. More than 600 links to physical activity/sports organizations and associations.

RUNNING FREEBIES AND OTHER CHEAP THRILLS

Health Analysis and Runner Survey

To join 55,000 runners in an ongoing Internet National Runner's Health Study go to www.healthsurvey.org. This study by a researcher at Lawrence Berkeley National Laboratory is evaluating how much running is beneficial, whether running faster or further is better, the helpfulness of diet or dietary supplements, and other health-related issues.

There is no fee and runners who enter personal data receive an automatic, on-the-spot analysis of their diet, physical activity, and weight. Participants will also be recontacted periodically to update information and report their current health status.

If you don't have Internet access contact:

Paul Williams
National Runner's Health Study
Lawrence Berkeley National Laboratory
1 Cyclotron Road, Building 934
Berkeley, CA 94720-0001

Estimate Race Time, Pace, or Distance

To estimate what time you can run at one distance from a race time at another distance, use the Race Time Calculator under training and racing at www.runnersworld.com.

Use WinRun at www.ourworld.compuserve.com/homepages/ RoyWeinberg to calculate your pace, run time, or distance by using two of these three factors.

Determine Fitness, Calorie Usage, and Body Mass

Using personal data like weight, sex, and age, calculate the number of calories burned while running different distances with the Calorie Calculator: www.stevenscreek.com/goodies.

Calculate your body mass index at www.shapeup.org. Web site of ShapeUp America, a nonprofit organization founded by former U.S. Surgeon General C. Everett Koop.

Go to www.fitnesszone.com to figure your "Free Fitness Profile" by answering a series of questions about nutrition, exercise, and health.

Freeware and Shareware

Free and low-cost computer tools for runners are available from:

Running Works
Box 6030
Huntsville, AL 35824
E-mail: Dazzlesoft@aol.com
Web site: www.catalog.com/webrun/running/runworks

Exercise Log (for Macintosh)
c/o Maurits van der Veen
Department of Government
Harvard University, GSAS
Cambridge, MA 02138
E-mail: maurits@fas.harvard.edu
Web site: www.fas.harvard.edu/~maurits/ExerciseLog.html

WinRunLog
Web site: www.ourworld.compuserve.com/homepages/Roy Weinberg

Interactive Running Widgets

Links to more than seventy interactive running tools, charts, and calculators: www.runnersweb.com/running/rw_widg.html.

Free Subscriptions

Runner's Niche, an on-line, noncommercial E-magazine dedicated to runners: www.home.netone.com/~woodyg3/runiche

Don't Stop Moving, a free on-line newsletter with training advice, inspiration, and running info:

Perpetual Motion
PO Box 1605
Bend, OR 97709
Phone: (541) 330-5836
E-mail: pmotion@teleport.com
Web site: www.teleport.com/~pmotion/index.html

Jeff Galloway's Newsletter, containing training tips for all levels of runners:

Galloway Productions
4651 Roswell Rd., Suite I-802
Atlanta, GA 30342
Phone: 1-800-200-2771
Fax: (404) 252-3971
E-mail: gallowayprod@mindspring.com
Web site: www.jeffgalloway.com

Free samples

Free samples or trial issues of the following newsletters are available by sending a self-addressed, stamped (55¢) envelope to:

Running and FitNews
American Running and Fitness Association
4405 East West Hwy., Suite 405
Bethesda, MD 20814
Phone: 1-800-776-ARFA
Fax: (301) 913-9520
E-mail: arfarun@aol.com
Web site: www.arfa.org

The Fitness Monitor
2636 Fulton Ave., Suite 100
Sacramento, CA 95821
Phone: (916) 451-7043
E-mail: bltfitness@aol.com
Web site: http://members.aol.com/bltfitness/tfm.htm

National Run to Work Day

Each year in the fall, the Road Runners Club of America and runners around the country celebrate National Run to Work Day to promote the benefits of running, safety on the roads and trails, and environmental awareness. Run the entire way to work or creatively combine running with other modes of transportation. Call (703) 836-0558 or visit www.rrca.org for more information.

For unfamiliar terms used in the definitions below look for entries elsewhere in this glossary.

Achilles: *Tendon* that connects the calf to the heel.

aerobic: In the presence of or with oxygen.

aerobic capacity: Body's maximum ability to use oxygen to produce energy during exercise. Also known as VO_2max.

all-comers meet: Informal track meet for participants of all ages and abilities.

anaerobic: Without oxygen.

anaerobic threshold: Point during high-*intensity* exercise when demands for oxygen are more than the heart and lungs can provide.

base: Foundation of aerobic training and endurance that prepares the body for demands of higher intensity training.

calisthenics: Exercises that build muscle endurance by using body weight. Examples include sit-ups, lunges and push-ups.

calories (kilocalorie, kcal): Unit of energy. Commonly-used to express the fuel or energy value of food.

capillary beds: Small vessels between arteries and veins where oxygen, nutrients, as well as, wastes are exchanged.

carbohydrates: Essential *nutrients*. Body's most readily available source of energy. One gram of carbohydrates equals four *calories*.

cardiac drift: Normal response of the heart that occurs primarily as the result of *dehydration* or loss of body fluids. The heart gradually beats faster (*heart rate* increases) even though pace or exercise *intensity* remains constant.

cardiovascular: Pertaining to the heart and blood vessels.

cool-down: Low-*intensity* exercise at the end of a workout or race that aids the body in recovering to its pre-exercise state.

cross-training: Training in more than one sport or activity. Used to improve overall fitness and reduce the risk of injuries and *overtraining* in the primary sport.

dehydration: Physical state when the body contains less than an optimal amount of *water*.

endorphins: Chemicals in the central nervous system that influence the perception of pain and produces feeling of euphoria during vigorous exercise. Also see *runner's high*.

endurance: Important component of fitness. Ability of the body to resist fatigue.

fat: Essential *nutrient* that provides stored energy. One gram of fat equals nine *calories*.

fartlek: Swedish word for "speed play." Unstructured, interval-like, speed training.

flexibility: Important component of fitness. The ability to move safely and comfortably through a required range of motion.

F.I.T. principle: Training concept utilizing three inter-related components—*frequency*, *intensity* and *time*—to determine the exercise doseage required to maintain or improve fitness.

frequency: Component of the *F.I.T. principle* which refers to the number of days per week that you train or exercise.

fun run: Short, low-key running events or races.

footstrike: Way the foot makes contact with the ground. Most distance runners are "heel strikers."

gait: Movement of running.

glucose: A simple sugar. Body's principle source of energy.

glycogen: Form of *glucose* that is stored primarily in the muscles and liver. Used for energy during *aerobic* activity.

hamstrings: Group of muscles located on the back of the thigh.

hash: Playful running event held throughout the world by groups of runners who call themselves "the drinking club with a running problem."

heart rate: Number of times an individual's heart beats per minute.

hill training: Training conducted on hills and used to develop leg strength.

inflammation: Body's response to injury or infection generally characterized by redness, swelling and/or pain.

intensity: Component of the *F.I.T. principle* which refers to the amount of force or effort exerted during exercise.

interval training: Type of *speedwork* involving short, high-intensity exercise periods separated by periods of rest or low-intensity exercise. It increases leg speed and improves cardiorespiratory fitness.

lactic acid: Waste product of *anaerobic* energy production that accumulates during high-*intensity* exercise and causes fatigue.

ligament: Connective tissue that hold the bones together at the joints.

long slow distance (LSD): Type of low-intensity running done for long duration.

marathon: Popular running race that is 26 miles, 385 yards, or approximately 26.2 miles.

maximum heart rate (Max HR): Maximum number of times an individual's heart beats in one minute. It is genetically-determined, sports-specific, and can not be increased with training.

minerals: Inorganic compounds that serve a variety of important functions in the body. Examples include iron, calcium, potassium, and sodium.

nutrients: Components of food needed by the body.

"one-paceitis": Tongue-in-cheek condition of runners who always run the same pace and have difficulty altering their pace.

orthotics: Shoe inserts designed to correct faulty foot biomechanics.

osteoporosis: A disease of severe bone loss. Risk can be reduced through weight-bearing exercise like running.

overload: Training principle that challenges the body's current level of fitness by stressing it more than usual. To be effective, recovery or rest must follow periods of overload.

overpronation: Excessive inward roll of the foot before push-off. Frequent cause of running injuries.

overstride: Improper lengthening of the stride that forces the foot to land in front of the knee.

overtraining: Condition of extreme mental and/or physical fatigue that occurs when the body is unable to adapt to repeated stress of *training*. Usually the result of inadequate rest and recovery.

oxygen debt: Stage during high *intensity* exercise when the body uses oxygen faster than it can deliver it to the working muscles.

personal record: Individual's best time for a specific race distance or course. Also known as PR or personal best.

pronation: Natural, normal motion when the foot rolls inward then flattens out before toeing off.

protein: Essential nutrient that helps rebuild and repair the body. One gram of protein equals four *calories*.

quadriceps: Group of large muscles on the front of the thigh.

repetition (rep): Common speed and strength training term. The number of times an exercise is performed or an *interval* is run.

RICE: Acronym for a treatment of minor injuries—rest, ice, compression and elevation.

runner's high: Difficult-to-describe feeling of effortless running that some runner's experience and others believe is non-existent.

set: Common speed and strength training term. Group of *repetitions* or *reps.*

specificity: Theory that training must be sport-specific or system and muscle-specific for optimal performance.

speed work: Component of training that emphasizes running fast—at goal race pace or even slightly faster. *Intervals* are an example.

sprain: Injury to a *ligament*. Complete or partial tear that occurs by stretching a ligament past its limit or range.

strain: Injury to a muscle which occurs from overuse or stretching beyond its limit or range.

supination: Uncommon motion when the foot rolls outward. Also known as underpronation.

talk test: Subjective technique which measures exercise intensity based on the ability to carry on a conversation while running or exercising.

tempo run: Hard, steady-state run done at near race pace but for a shorter than race distance.

tendons: Connective issue at the ends of the muscle that attach muscle to bone.

"terrible too's": Common cause of running injuries—too much, too soon, too far, too fast.

time: Component of the *F.I.T. principle* which refers to the duration of a given workout.

training: Systematic and comprehensive program designed to prepare the body for a specific goal or objective.

training effect: Generic term which applies to a variety of physical and mental changes that occur as the body adapts to the demands of *training*.

ultramarathon: Foot race that is longer than 26.2 miles. Also known as an ultra.

visualization: Training technique using mental images.

vitamins: Organic substances that are necessary for normal functioning of the body.

VO$_2$max: Scientific term for the maximum amount of oxygen that can be consumed in one minute. Also known as *aerobic capacity* and maximum oxygen update.

"the Wall": Invisible roadblock created by a shortage of *glycogen* and/or the limits of a runner's *training*. Characterized by extreme fatigue and an overwhelming urge to slow down dramatically or stop running.

warm-up: Low intensity exercise at the beginning of a workout or before a race which prepares the body physiologically and psychologically for the higher *intensity* exercise that follows.